KT-571-236

To

ELSPETH MAUREEN

who kept the translator to it

CONTENTS

INTRODUCTION

CAMOENS' poem, the national epic of Portugal, is the story of a
people – numbering then perhaps a million and a quarter – who in
the space of a century and a quarter spread over the waters of the
globe, carried their flag and their faith from Brazil to Japan, and
established not merely an empire but a new conception of empire
based on mastery of the ocean routes. 'God gave the Portuguese a
small country as cradle but all the world as their grave,' wrote
António Vieira in the seventeenth century. If they temporarily ex-
hausted themselves in the process, they left the world as seen from
Europe a very different place, and the whole course of subsequent
history bears the imprint. *The Lusiads* is more, however, than the
mere narrative of that achievement: it is also an interpretation of
the underlying greatness of those who achieved it, and as such the
best possible introduction to Portugal and the Portuguese. Being
conceived in essentially poetic terms, it may fittingly be prefaced
by a brief account in prosaic chronological sequence of the more
notable landmarks in the long heroic story.

It was an important differential factor in the Peninsula that,
whereas Spain did not recover full possession of her territory from
the Moslem invader until the fall of Granada in 1492, after a
struggle lasting close on eight hundred years, the Reconquest to
Portugal was the preoccupation of less than two centuries and was
completed by 1267. Portuguese prowess at sea had already won its
spurs in the extension of the fighting in its closing stages to the
waters of the Atlantic; and the fact that in succeeding centuries the
fight for survival was to be against Spain did not obscure the per-
sisting threat to the faith from across the Strait.

With the infidel so close at hand, the crusades to the Holy Land had not engaged Portugal directly. Indirectly she benefited on occasion by the touching at her ports of valiant knights-errant from north-western Europe on their way to Palestine by sea, and English crusaders played a notable part in the taking of Lisbon from the Moslem in 1147. Some of these went no further: one, Gilbert of Hastings, became first Bishop of Lisbon. Crusading in the Peninsula was recognized by Rome to be fully as meritorious as crusading elsewhere, and such had been the fervour Portugal engendered in the process that even after the expulsion of the infidel she remained persuaded of her mission to continue the challenge and, in the name of the Church militant, to carry the war into Africa.

Here England comes into the picture once more. In 1385, 500 English archers in the pay of John of Gaunt did yeoman service on the field of Aljubarrota, which put an end to Spanish designs on Portugal for the next 200 years. In 1386 the Treaty of Windsor bound England to Portugal – which enjoys thereby the status of our oldest ally – 'for ever'. And in 1387 Philippa of Lancaster, John of Gaunt's daughter, married João I, the first of the House of Aviz, to become by him the mother of the most famous royal family in Portuguese history. It was this Anglo-Portuguese line of Aviz that formally launched Portugal on the high seas and blazed the trail of empire. All five sons took part, with their father, in the capture of Ceuta in 1415. This was the country's first overseas expedition, that Philippa had blessed from her death-bed, and in her third son Henrique, known to English readers as Henry the Navigator, it stirred a vision which was never to forsake him thereafter.

Withdrawing from the Court, Henrique established at Lagos on the south coast a centre for maritime research and exploration on an ever-increasing scale, drawing to his employ captains, pilots, cartographers and scientists and dispatching annual expeditions of discovery. The Mediterranean was known already, and the north coast of Africa. In addressing himself to the Atlantic and the west coast Henrique was guided by a variety of motives, scientific, religious, diplomatic, commercial. He sought communication and if possible an alliance with the mysterious Prester John, ruler of a Christian Ethiopia; he sought new channels of trade for his country; he sought to discover, perhaps to annex and colonize, new lands; he sought to extend the Christian faith at the expense of Mohammedanism; and, ultimate objective of all, he sought a sea route to India and the East. There too, as in Ethiopia, there existed the possibility of Christian allies, in the St Thomas's Christians so-called of the Malabar coast, and this crusader's vision of a grand strategy that would take the Mohammedan world in the rear was given official recognition in Papal bulls.

The East also meant spices, the most sought-after commodity of the Middle Ages. It was their seasoning that made tolerable through long winter months the salt beef killed of necessity each autumn; they added flavour to a diet infinitely more restricted and monotonous at the best of times than that of today; in medical practice they were credited with many rare virtues and potencies. Pepper, cloves, cinnamon, nutmeg, mace, aloes, ginger, camphor, incense and the various aromatic woods, these had been the key to the wealth first of Constantinople, then of Venice. Carried in Moslem vessels up the Persian Gulf or the Red Sea, by camel across Turkey and Egypt to Tripolis and Alexandria, to Italy in Venetian or Genoese galleys, they were distributed thence over Europe at a price commensurate with the journey. Untold riches awaited the European nation that could secure direct access to the sources of supply, a reward enhanced by the intense religious satisfaction to be derived from seeing the enemies of the faith lose control over so lucrative a traffic. It was not so much Venice which held the gorgeous East in fee as the Moslems the West.

By the time of Henrique's death in 1460 the West African mainland was known as far as Cape Palmas, where the coast turns due east to form the Gulf of Guinea, while Madeira, the Canary Islands and the Azores had all been colonized. His last expedition, to Alcácer-Seguer, near Tangier, in 1458, serves to underline the crusading zeal that was never absent from Portuguese expansion. Its success was to fire a succession of monarchs – Afonso V, João II, Manoel I – with the ambition to found an empire in Morocco, and to that extent it thwarted the progress of discovery to the south.

The next impetus came from a new direction. In 1487 João II fathered two very divergent undertakings with the same specific objectives of discovering Prester John and reaching India. The first was the mission of Pero da Covilhã to the East by way of the Mediterranean and the Red Sea. At Aden Covilhã took passage in a 'Mecca ship' that deposited him a month later – it was the summer now of 1488 – in Cananor. He had reached India, the first Portuguese to do so. From there he visited Calicut, the great centre of Indian trade with the West, which he found to be largely in the hands of Moslems, and Goa, a mart for the supply chiefly of Arabian horses.

Returning by way of Ormuz, Covilhã now sailed down the east coast of Africa as far as Sofala, where again he found Arabs in possession of the trade in gold from the interior. In 1493, after several years of further journeying in Arabia and Persia, he set foot in Abyssinia and found his Prester John, whose importance as an ally against the Moslem does not appear to have come up to expectations. Meanwhile he had duly reported to Lisbon on his earlier travels. Their importance lay, not in confirmation of the wealth of the East, but in the conviction his visit to Sofala had given him that the sea route from Lisbon was feasible.

The gap in knowledge still remaining was filled in most opportunely by the second enterprise aforementioned, that had been set on foot only a few months after that of Covilhã. This was the memorable voyage of Bartolomeu Dias, which gave at last the answer to the great query whether Africa could in fact be rounded to the south. Thanks to a store-ship, Dias's two small caravels were able to undertake a much longer voyage than any hitherto contemplated. Even so he had full measure, for once past the Congo strong winds drove him south for so long that when at length he was able to tack about he had already rounded the Cape without knowing it, and struck land at what is now known as Mossel Bay. Following the new and so exciting trend of the coastline, he reached the Great Fish River.

Another few days' sailing would have taken him to Sofala, over two years before Covilhã was to reach it, and between them they would have circumnavigated the continent; but his men had had enough, and compelled him to return home. The buffeting Dias received as he now rounded the Cape to the west led him to baptize it the Cape of Storms. King João, alive to the full significance of the achievement, renamed it the Cape of Good Hope. And now the stage was set for the greatest venture of all, that was to mark the culmination of a century of highly intelligent and infinitely courageous maritime endeavour.

This was reserved to Manoel 'the Fortunate', who came to the throne in 1495. His choice for leader of the expedition fell on Vasco da Gama, a gentleman of the royal household possessed of some nautical experience, who, on 8 July 1497, weighed anchor with two square-rigged, shallow-draught three-masters of some two hundred tons each by our reckoning, built under the supervision of Bartolomeu Dias, an older lateen-rigged caravel of half the size, and a store-ship of perhaps four hundred tons. For armament they carried twenty guns, including several breech-loaders. The officers wore armour and carried swords, the men leather jerkins and breastplates, with crossbows, axes and pikes. They were 170 in all, among them some who had already sailed with Dias; a dozen convicts were at the Captain's disposal for any particularly dangerous undertaking. One in three of the crews was fated to fall victim to scurvy and never see Portugal again.

Fogs and storms, calms, currents and contrary winds were for long the mariners' portion. Standing out to sea after leaving the Cape Verdes, they did not sight land again for ninety-six days, when they found themselves still some days' sail north of the Cape. This proved once more the Cape of Storms: not until four days after sighting it were they able to make their way beyond. Three days later, in Mossel Bay, they broke up the store-ship, and after another eight days passed Dias's farthest north, the Great Fish River. Natal they reached on Christmas Day, hence the name. Only in this region, as yet, were they strictly speaking explorers. From Sofala northward, for so long as they held to the coast, they would be treading in Covilhã's footsteps, in regions moreover where Arab traders, carrying with them something of Moslem civilization, had tempered the native savagery.

To da Gama this latter change was not for the better, since he had to contend henceforth with the treachery of enemies who were immediately alive to the threat to their interests. In Mozambique, and again in Mombasa, he narrowly escaped destruction through their plottings. Malindi, farther north, brought a kindlier reception, though da Gama had now learnt his lesson and refused to go ashore. It brought too – his greatest need – a pilot who could guide him over the last and most hazardous lap of all, that Indian Ocean that no vessel from the West had ever sailed before. Twenty-three days after leaving the African coast the sailors had their first glimpse of India in the Ghats, and on 20 May 1498 they dropped anchor off Calicut. The voyage had lasted ten and a half months. And now East and West had met, without intermediary. A new era in history was about to begin.

Columbus's New World may have loomed larger to Europe since. At the turn of the fifteenth century da Gama's discovery was held much the greater, and with reason. For the spices and precious stones he brought back from India symbolized not merely the ruin of Venice, the turning of the Mediterranean into a backwater, and the emergence of Portugal, a country insignificant in size and population, as the richest nation in Europe. They held in kernel too the opening up of two unknown continents, Africa and Asia, and the discovery of a third, Australia. They heralded, finally, the revolutionizing of men's ideas of empire, the old basis of territorial conquest suffering eclipse with the development of trade and sea-power. On these were to soar to pinnacles of greatness till then undreamt-of first Portugal, then Holland, and lastly England, nations all three that otherwise might well have left but little mark on history. Manoel proclaimed himself grandiloquently 'Lord of the Conquest, Navigation and Commerce of Ethiopia, Arabia, Persia, and India'.

There remained to the sixteenth century the task of exploitation and consolidation. Since trade, not territory, was the material objective, the fleets that followed in the wake of da Gama were concerned to establish, first, friendly relations wherever possible with local potentates and peoples, and secondly, a chain of trading posts and fortresses for the better ordering of their maritime traffic and for defence against their Moslem rivals.

The next expedition, that of Pedro Alvares Cabral, left Lisbon six months to the day after da Gama's return. Sailing first to Brazil – tradition has long had it that the fleet, driven off its course by contrary winds, then first discovered this new land, though there are grounds for thinking that others of their nation may have been there before – Cabral took formal possession in his sovereign's name and continued on his way. Four of his thirteen vessels foundered in a storm near the Cape, Dias its discoverer being among the victims; only six were to reach their goal. In India Moslem hostility led this time to fighting, and Cabral's bombardment of Calicut forfeited to the Portuguese thereafter the friendship of its ruler or Samorin. In 1502 da Gama returned with fifteen vessels, and detailed a squadron to remain for the defence of the trading stations that had been set up at Cochin and Cananor. Duarte Pacheco, left on land with a small force in the following year, defeated the Samorin on the field seven times over, as well as destroying his fleet, and laid the foundations of Portuguese military and naval prestige in the East.

The changing situation was reflected in the dispatch in 1504 of Francisco de Almeida with a force of 2,500 men, of whom 1,500 were soldiers. Almeida was the first to rank as Viceroy and to set up a formal government, with seat at Cochin, for the bases the Portuguese now held. Before long the Sultan of Egypt was in the fray, not without incitement from Venice, and there ensued an encounter off Diu in 1508 which resulted in a resounding victory for the Portuguese and proclaimed them undisputed masters of the Indian Ocean.

Afonso de Albuquerque, Almeida's successor in 1509 and the greatest of the Viceroys, who had already conquered Ormuz and made of the Persian Gulf another Portuguese preserve, cast the shadow of his might over the Red Sea too. It was he who in 1510 seized Goa, thereafter the centre of Portuguese dominion in the

East, and sought to colonize it by encouraging his men to marry natives and settle permanently.

Soon, as though India and the Indian Ocean were not enough, these mariners from the Tagus began prospecting across the Bay of Bengal and into the China Sea. Malacca, taken in 1511, not merely controlled all traffic with this new Farther East: it led directly to contact with Siam, Java, Cochin China and the Moluccas or Spice Islands, the first reports of whose wealth threatened to cast even da Gama's achievement into the shade and were the direct motive of Magalhães' voyage of circumnavigation of the globe (1519–22) that gave the Philippine Islands to Spain. By then various Portuguese embassies and trading missions had been in touch with China. In 1542 one such was caught in a typhoon and so battered that for fifteen days it drifted at the mercy of the winds, which carried it to Japan. This was their farthest north, Timor and New Guinea their farthest south; it is not impossible that some may have skirted the coast of Australia.

Other travellers, Jesuits for the most part, penetrated even more heroically into the unknown by land, and without the lure of material reward. One found his way to Tibet, another spent five years on an overland journey from India to China. All the world was their parish, and it was they and not the traders who turned the discovery of Japan to account in pursuit of that second but never merely secondary of the two objectives on which Portugal was now spending herself so recklessly. One exploit, this time to the west, deserves particular mention. In 1541 Ethiopia was delivered from her Moslem enemies, 'saved', as Gibbon placed on record, 'by 450 Portuguese', and is still today a Christian country.

João de Castro, who reached Goa in 1545, was the last of the great Viceroys. Where Albuquerque laid the foundations, he completed the edifice of empire. In retrospect the year of his death, 1548, could be seen to mark the apogee of Portuguese greatness in the East. Camoens so saw it, and ended his account of his country's achievement in India with his name. Alike at home and in the East the new wealth was already taking its toll of the nation's stamina in lassitude and corruption. The fundamental weakness lay in the impossible drain of an enterprise so infinite in scale upon the country's severely limited resources in man-power. The yearly expeditions to the East were sapping its life-blood.

At length, in 1578, King Sebastião administered the death-blow with his ill-fated crusade to North Africa. Within two years Portugal and her empire had fallen into the lap of Spain, and disintegration set in straightway with the invitation to Spain's chief enemies, England and Holland, to attack that empire wherever on the broad seas opportunity offered. That Portugal did not recover all with the recovery of independence in 1640 is not the wonder, but rather that she recovered so much. For even without the events of 1578 Portugal, so successful in warding off the Moslem powers of the East, could not have counted for much longer on passive acquiescence in her monopoly from the other Christian powers of the West. 'I should very much like,' remarked Francis I of France, 'to see the clause in Adam's will that excludes me from a share of the world.'

THE POET

The basic facts in the story of Camoens' life are three: he was a representative product of his age and nation; in *The Lusiads* he wrote an epic at once vibrant with patriotic pride and instinct with experience and emotion; and, if not indeed from the cradle, from early manhood to the grave he knew in fullest measure the buffetings that fortune is reputed to heap with predilection on poetic genius. From every material point of view his life was one long plumbing of the depths of frustration and failure.

Luis Vaz de Camões was born, most probably in Lisbon, about the year 1524, the year in which Vasco da Gama died. His family, Galician in origin, ranked among the lesser nobility. From his grandfather's marriage into that of the da Gamas the poet had inherited a personal interest in the great discovery, and a still nearer link with India and the hazards of the journey thither was provided by his father, Simão Vaz de Camões, who went to the East as ship's captain, was wrecked off Goa and, having been rescued on a plank, there died. The young Luis went in due course to the ancient university which, having several times perambulated between Coimbra and the capital, was in 1537 transferred definitively to that delightful city on the Mondego, ever the chosen abode of the Muses in Portugal.

This was the fair morning of the Renaissance in Portugal as elsewhere. Greek and Latin studies, enthusiastically accepted as the key to a new world not of knowledge merely but of the imagination, were effecting a re-birth in Portuguese poetry. Whether Camoens came to know much of Greek literature at first hand is doubtful. His thorough grounding in Latin, and in the mythology and history of the ancients in general, is not open to question, nor his responsiveness to the newer poetry of the modern literatures. In Spanish, like many of his compatriots, he both read and composed. Among the Italians he knew Petrarch, Boiardo, Ariosto. These years on the banks of the Mondego, drinking in the world's great poetry and essaying his own poetic wings, were doubtless the happiest of his life.

About 1544 he returned to Lisbon, where for several years he frequented Court and aristocratic circles, still writing poetry and venturing now into the field of comedy as well. A hopeless love affair, that left a deep impress on his heart and verse, led to banishment from the capital – whether self-imposed or by royal decree is a matter of interpretation – in 1546. In the following year he went to Ceuta as a common soldier, and his real life had begun. It was appropriate that one whose whole future was to be bound up with the vicissitudes of a far-flung empire should begin his experience in the very cradle of the imperial adventure; and the loss there of his right eye brought vividly home to him the price that the adventure entailed. Empire he was to see always thereafter, not as the impersonal achievement of a nation, but in terms of individual character, heroism and devotion, the aggregate of personal qualities the decay of which must inevitably spell collapse.

The Camoens who returned to Lisbon in 1549 bore the stamp upon him of a rough-and-tumble world. He had turned self-assertive, provocative with tongue and sword; and the upshot of a street brawl on Corpus Christi Day, 1552, in which he wounded a Court official, was a prison sentence, followed nine months later by a royal pardon on the understanding that he should go to serve the king in India. And for India, in May 1553, he sailed. This was good-bye to, not the threshold of, the career he had looked for. 'I set out,' he wrote, 'as one leaving this world for the next.' Seventeen years were to pass before he would see his native country again, a penniless and broken man for all his genius.

Of the four ships that sailed for Goa that year, his, the *São Bento*, was the only one to arrive. On the return voyage it too was wrecked. For him also the Cape of Good Hope proved still the Cape of Storms, and the atmosphere of Goa itself, that 'grave of honest poverty', he was to find heavy with disillusion. Activity at least he did not lack. Within six weeks of his arrival he was engaged in an expedition against the King of Chembe, down the Malabar coast. Tradition associates him with other engagements against enemy shipping in the Red Sea and off the shores of Arabia in the following year.

Meanwhile the poet in him was already looking beneath the surface of peril and adventure for the inner reality of empire, and some of his satirical poems written about this time may well have said more than officialdom was anxious to hear. 'This Babylon, whence flows matter for every evil the world breeds . . ., where tyranny overrides honour . . .; this labyrinth where nobility, valour and learning go begging at the portals of avarice and meanness . . .' The epic days were already over. And what remained was not pleasant to contemplate.

Camoens had his friends in high places: this much his years at Court still meant to him. They included more than one of the eight Viceroys or Governors-General under whom he served, and his appointment in 1556 to the post of Trustee for the Dead and Absent in distant Macau, where two years previously China had consented to the establishment of a Portuguese settlement, was lucrative and acceptable enough, whether or not it is to be taken as yet another decree of exile for indiscretion. On the way to Macau he appears to have visited not merely Malacca, a normal port of call, but the Moluccas, and to have tarried there for perhaps a year.

But fate was still hostile. In Macau his duties led to friction with the settlers, and within a year or two he was relieved of his post and sent back to Goa. If in chains, as tradition has it, these were to prove but a transitory affliction; for somewhere near the mouth of the Mekong River the vessel made shipwreck. Camoens escaped with his life, clutching tight the drenched and still unfinished manuscript of his epic. Whatever wealth he had come by in Macau lay at the bottom of the China Sea.

Back in Goa in 1561, there ensued a further six years in India concerning which a brief period in prison on the matter of his administration in Macau and another, or the threat of another, for debt are our nearest approaches to knowledge. By now he was desirous of returning home. The country that had earlier seemed to spurn him – 'Ingrata patria', he had vowed, 'non possidebis ossa mea' – was still his motherland, and in so far as he still knew ambition it was to see his *Lusiads* in print and to bask in the warmth of whatever appreciation it might evoke.

But a soldier shipped to India at the royal expense returned at his own, and not until a friendly captain appointed to the command of Sofala offered to take him as far as Mozambique could Camoens leave Goa. It was now September 1567. The journey out had taken six months. Inured as he was to misfortune, he could little have dreamt that the home-coming would take five times as long. There was no second friendly captain to repeat the favour from Mozambique, and there the poet languished for two long years, tholing penury and ill-health we know not how, sustaining himself spiritually by working away at his magnum opus. The historian Diogo do Couto, returning home late in 1569 and himself forced by bad weather to winter in Mozambique, found his friend there engaged further in compiling a *Parnasso de Luis de Camões*, a book, he tells us, 'rich in learning, doctrine and philosophy'. He and others came to the rescue, and between them defrayed the cost of the journey to Lisbon. Ill-luck was still in attendance; the *Parnasso* was stolen, and never heard of more.

Disembarking in the Tagus in April 1570, Camoens found Lisbon just emerging from a devastating visitation of the plague. He had the impression that his country had altered much, and for the worse. The native virtues of the race appeared to him to have wilted under prosperity, people at home not realizing at what cost of blood, sweat and tears their empire had been built. The structure had doubtless been reared on too scanty foundations: important sectors of opinion had been against it from the beginning. Now the heroic temper, the will to rise to the magnitude of the challenge, was ebbing; and this fundamental irresponsibility, that existed at all levels, Camoens found strongest precisely at the top, in the counsels of the boy-king Sebastião who two years before, in 1568, had assumed the reins of power at the mature age of fourteen.

It was in this mood of disillusion that Camoens now penned to his monarch the Prologue-dedicatory and the Epilogue to his poem, seeking valiantly to keep alive in his own breast and to fire in others the hope that the nation, wisely led, still had it in its power to be what it had been and to provide the stuff of epics yet unwritten. The poem was passed by the censor and granted the royal licence for publication in 1571; it appeared in 1572.

Little immediate recognition was forthcoming, beyond a modest pension granted by the king for a term of three years that, twice renewed, was to be continued after his death to his aged mother. 'The sufficiency he showed in the book he wrote concerning the affairs of India' was how Sebastião had appraised *The Lusiads*. If there was scant honour here for poet or patriot, it was all the poet was to receive in his own country. None of his other writings, if we except some commendatory verses penned for the works of friends, was published in his lifetime. As for the patriot, the gathering clouds which darkened his closing years concerned precisely the 'sufficiency' of Sebastião himself. India, unlike Africa, had brought returns material as well as to the faith, and a monarch like João III had been realist enough, when compelled to choose, to abandon between 1542 and 1550 four of the eight North African strongholds. Sebastião was an idealist and a religious crusader with a soul above such mercenary pursuits as the navigation and commerce of any region anywhere. The day came when he too had to choose, and he chose Africa.

The expedition Sebastião led in person to Alcácer-Kebir in June 1578 totalled some 15,000 foot and 1,500 horse, with 9,000 camp-followers of every description. Five hundred vessels were needed to transport it. Such a force in India, wisely led, could have held the Portuguese banner aloft all over the East for many a long year. In a four-hour engagement with the Moors, under an African sun, it melted to nothing. Eight thousand were killed, 15,000 more taken and sold as slaves; possibly 100 in all succeeded in reaching the coast and safety. Sebastião was among the slain, having laid the might and prestige of Portugal in the dust.

Towards the close of 1579 the plague again descended on Lisbon. Camoens lay ill, broken in body and spirit. He no longer had the will to live, and from what he knew was his death-bed he wrote to a friend: 'All will see that so dear to me was my country that I was content to die not only in but with it.' He died on 10 June 1580, spared at least the ignominy of seeing Philip II of Spain cross the frontier as king of a united Peninsula. In this alone was fate kind to him. His mother survived him: with her – for he had had neither brother, sister, wife, nor child – his line became extinct. Three hundred years later, in 1880, his presumed remains were removed to the church at Belem that Manoel the Fortunate had built to celebrate the discovery of the sea route to India, on the same spot whence da Gama sailed and to which he returned. There they keep company with those of da Gama himself, his distant kinsman and hero.

THE POEM

Os Lusíadas means the sons of Lusus, companion of Bacchus and mythical first settler in Portugal: hence, the Portuguese. Virgil, to the Renaissance the greatest among the poets of antiquity, had sung of arms and the man. The *Aeneid* was to Camoens at once model and challenge, but from the opening words he made clear

THE POEM

that his would be an *Aeneid* with a difference. 'Arms and the men' was his theme, the epic exaltation of a whole race of heroes. What Portugal had accomplished in the East was incomparably greater than the heroic themes of antiquity – and it was true. Nor was it great merely in isolation, the achievement of a handful of stalwarts. It had a national significance, for those stalwarts were the product of all their country's past, and the enterprise was itself but the coping-stone of the logic of that past. And it boasted an even wider significance still, inasmuch as Portugal was engaged in a fight for the true faith, for the spiritual values of Europe, against the forces of error and darkness. It was against this double background that the heroic narrative had to be set, thus involving a range alike in time and in space greater than the career of any one hero could span.

Camoens' tale centres, like the *Aeneid*, on a storm-tossed mariner who ventures into the unknown to the founding of a second Roman Empire, and it is by devices largely borrowed from Virgil that this problem of interweaving past, present and future is solved. Thus Jupiter in Canto 2 reveals to Venus the brilliant destiny reserved to da Gama and to those who are to follow. Throughout Cantos 3 and 4 da Gama is himself relating to the King of Malindi his country's story. Canto 5, a continuance of the same narrative, is the story of his own voyage from Lisbon, inasmuch as the fleet, when we first meet it in Canto 1, has already rounded the Cape and is sailing up the east coast of Africa. The reason for this apparently arbitrary plunge *in medias res* is evident. Da Gama's voyage is the artistic fulcrum of the poem, but his proud and oft-repeated claim to be sailing through seas none had sailed before only begins to be valid at the point where Bartolomeu Dias had turned back. His experiences in covering the same ground are accordingly told in retrospect, with the briefest of indications, on coming to the spot in question, that others had been there before.

It is here, in Canto 5, that we meet one of the most original episodes in the poem, the encounter with the giant Adamastor, personifying the Cape of Storms, who predicts the dire vengeance he will wreak on subsequent over-confiding violators of his territorial waters. In Canto 7 we have the counterpart of Aeneas's shield. The Catual or Governor of Calicut is intrigued by the heroic scenes depicted on the banners he sees on board da Gama's vessel, and his curiosity allows a recital, in some part reminiscent of Canto 3, of outstanding figures and incidents in the chequered past of Portugal.

Canto 10 is wholly given up to prediction. First a nymph foretells to da Gama the achievements in Africa, Egypt, Arabia, Persia, India, and Ceylon of the succession of sailors, soldiers, and administrators who are to follow up his discovery over the next half century; then Tethys the sea-goddess, taking him to the top of a high mountain, grants him, along with a bird's-eye glimpse of the world intended to fix in memory the places associated with the exploits already recounted, a preview of all the lands and islands of the Farther East the Portuguese were still to discover, Siam, Malacca, Sumatra, Borneo, the Moluccas, China, and Japan, rounding off the picture with a glimpse at Brazil in the Farther West.

Such is the machinery by which the whole of the Portuguese record at home and overseas is made to hinge on the central theme, and it becomes at once clear why *The Lusiads* is esteemed, and not only in Portugal, first as a poem, but also as an initiation into the entire history, polity and character of the Portuguese.

This brief analysis will also have thrown into relief an inherent contradiction in the conception, of which the poet was himself as well aware as the most carping of his critics. How justify, in a specifically Christian poem written to exalt a nation engaged in a centuries-long crusade for the faith, and studded of necessity with references to that faith and that crusade, the part here played by the gods and goddesses of pagan antiquity? Yet the answer is simple. For poetic purposes there could be no replacing the gods of Greece and Rome by God and his angels. These could never supply the counterpart of a Bacchus thumping and storming on Olympus at Jupiter's too obvious partiality for the Portuguese or descending to Neptune's under-water palace to state a case against their presumption, of a Venus breasting da Gama's vessel out of the

22

threats lurking in Mombasa harbour or contriving with Cupid's help the most sensuous of rewards for high endeavour.

The gods of antiquity were set above mortals, but not above their failings. They fell in and out of love, knew jealousy, temper, triumph and disappointment: to that extent they lived closer to mankind, interested themselves in men's interests, and took sides. A human issue could therefore be projected on to a higher, more symbolic level by imagining it as striking repercussions on Olympus. Whereas, moreover, God is the Supreme Power and all things obey his will, the gods were traditionally in large part but figurative interpretations of the mysterious and often conflicting forces of Nature; and the Portuguese achievement was at least as much a triumph over these as over human enemies. Adamastor by any Christian reckoning was but a headland. Let his figure stand as the measure of the imaginative gain *The Lusiads* derived throughout from Camoens' retention of classical myth.

There were other respects too in which the poet was quick to sense the deficiencies, for poetic purposes, of a purely historical presentation of the discovery, epic in nature and spirit as this was. Ercilla's *La Araucana* (1569–89), the finest of the various Spanish epics of overseas conquest, had been begun in the belief that the factual sufficed. 'I sing, not of ladies and love,' run the opening words, 'nor of the fond deeds of enamoured knights.' Soon, however, the author realized his mistake, and set himself to intertwine with the action imaginative episodes spun with preference around the tender passion. 'What good thing can there be,' he now asks, 'where love is not? What verse may, lacking love, still hope to please?' Da Gama's expedition had been a wholly male enterprise, and if the resulting monotony bore heavily on its members, Camoens foresaw that it would bear more heavily still on his readers, whose taste in the modern epic had been formed by Boiardo and Ariosto.

Hence three notable concessions, that by common consent are regarded as among the highlights of the poem, one purely lyrical, one chivalrous, one a gorgeous riot of the senses. The tragic fate of Inês de Castro, sacrificed to high policy because in her innocence she loved and was loved too well, had had its repercussions in Portuguese history; but that is not the justification for the loving detail that Camoens, once more for a moment the lyric and not the epic poet, lavishes upon the scene at such disproportionate length. Historical values are relative, poetic absolute, and for once he paused deliberately to redress the balance.

The story of the Twelve of England, more properly the Twelve who went to England, is told to beguile a chill early morning watch in the Indian Ocean. Advanced as a tale of derring-do, for 'soft topics are not for hard times like these', it still derives from the fair sex, being an illustration of what men will do to honour it as well as an encomium of Portuguese prowess. The origins of the theme are unknown. No reference to it in English record, understandably enough, has ever been discovered. Camoens had it from a contemporary romance of chivalry, and presents it as true. A good tale in itself, containing nothing incredible to such scorners of all the odds as were its hearers, and a proper reminder of the breed whence they were sprung as they drew near to that unknown land, their goal, where the lists would not be guaranteed, it was a reminder too of the gentler things of life that seemed now so far away, of gracious ladies and the refinements of conduct and ideals that their presence infused into society.

But it is the Island of Love above all that has engaged – and divided – the critics. Bacchus and the others may have but personified the forces of Nature on the outward journey. On the triumphant return Venus has the field to herself, and the colder sort of logic may well find it a trifle wanton that the reward for da Gama and his men – merchant-adventurers after spices but crusaders always at heart – should be a lovers' paradise where Tethys and her nymphs in all their loveliness are in league with Nature to minister to every indulgence the flesh is heir to. That it is all poetic fantasy goes without saying. The records of the voyage give no clue to this island that never was, and nothing is odder in the wide field of Camoens scholarship than the persisting theories of those who must locate it.

Camoens knew well enough how lame his explanation must

read that the island and its delights were but a feigning of 'the honours, delightful in themselves, that can make life sublime', and he may not escape the charge of having mingled two worlds and confused his effects. His mariners were greater than they knew and had achieved more than they knew: therein lay the lasting significance of his theme, and the reward ought to have been cast on the level of the achievement. Yet Camoens at heart was essentially a man of the Renaissance, not of the Counter-Reformation, as all his lyric poetry is there to prove, and he could not forgo the life of the senses. Nor, having treated his gods, abstractions, as men, could he now treat his men as abstractions. If his Portuguese were raised above the commonalty, they were still men, and in this sense his provision for them of the magic island is as realistic as anything else in the poem. 'What good thing can there be where love is not?' Its true figurative meaning – for it has this too – is the symbolizing in the marriage of mariners and nymphs of Portuguese mastery over the ocean.

But these are still extraneous beauties that adorn the poem, enhancing its charm and variety: they do not explain either its essential greatness or its serious intent. Camoens was a poet; he was also a thinker who had reflected long on the lessons that books and life had taught him. Not only can he see two sides of a question – and the old man who apostrophizes the fleet just before it sails from Lisbon could not have expressed his doubts and hesitations more convincingly had the poet's purpose been to decry instead of to laud the great adventure. Not only do we observe him constantly probing into character, seeking to assess the factors that spell greatness or decay and applying his analysis with even more insistence to the nation than to the individual. His scrutiny, as of one who oft at sea had strained his vision from the masthead, bent on piercing the enigma of the horizon, was concerned too with the larger problems of destiny and the meaning of existence.

Eloquent as *The Lusiads* is of the patriotism that chastises as lovingly as it applauds, its author, more than a Portuguese, is a European and a Christian, and these two concepts to him are interdependent. The Church militant, unless it be but cover for the pursuit of material advantage, must find its justification in the conviction that it is first, by divine revelation, the Church catholic; and how commend its catholicism to other lands and faiths if Europe itself be hesitant and rent in its support? Camoens pleads with the same sense of urgency as we do today the cause of a united Europe, with this difference, that the bases of the unity he pleads, and the advantages to be derived from it, are spiritual, not secular, and its grand objective is not defence but a crusade. Hence the series of meditative and hortatory passages, occurring for the most part at the end of Cantos, that have irked some readers as clogging the narrative.

Similar exception has been taken to Tethys' exposition of the magic globe with its Ptolemaic system of concentric spheres, though here the poet had his warrant to hand, at need, in Dante's *Paradiso*. His purpose is clear enough. Camoens did not need to be a mariner writing of mariners to feel the fascination of astronomy. The phenomena of terrestrial Nature were in his day the preserve of the scientist; the heavens were the perennial challenge to the philosopher, and as the progress of maritime discovery opened up more and more of the world the challenge became the more insistent to explain man's position in an ever-widening framework of relationships. The old concern over how Portugal stood to Spain had been dwarfed by the new and dramatic confrontation of Europe with Asia. And now, in the space of a generation, men from Portugal and Spain had sailed right round the world and the question, What next? transferred the issue from the physical to the metaphysical plane.

The Portuguese achievement, as Camoens saw it, was part of a great providential design to win the world for the true faith, the ulterior purpose of which clearly merged into God's purpose for the universe as a whole. It was not enough that his fellow-countrymen should feel pride in the material accomplishment: they must understand it in its wider setting. Ptolemy's system, still received in Camoens' time, was soon to receive a rude shock, and mankind a ruder, in the establishing that this earth was not after all the centre of creation, about which all the rest revolved. Yet its poetic truth remained, and remains, still largely intact. No greater incentive to high endeavour exists than the conviction that the individual is the centre of his universe and that it all depends on him.

Tethys' account of the stellar system having thus led back to earth, there follows a summary conspectus of the new and exciting regions, from Africa to Japan, that the exploitation of da Gama's initial discovery will shortly bring within the ken of western eyes. It is a double journey, outward by the coasts of the mainland, Abyssinia, Arabia, Persia, India – with here a long excursus, to relieve the catalogue, on St Thomas's miracles and martyrdom – Burma, Malaya, China; then back again by way of the islands that were so many pearls in the Portuguese diadem, Japan, the Moluccas, Borneo, Timor, Java, Sumatra, Ceylon, the Maldives, Socotra, Madagascar. If this smack to the modern reader of the class-room and the geography lesson, it is a reminder that to the sixteenth century there was, after the classics, no field of study, inside or outside the class-room, half so compelling. The sophistication of the modern age, weighed down with excess of knowledge concerning this so intractable planet of ours, can with difficulty recapture the sense of exaltation, constantly renewed, that added new dimensions to life as the curtain lifted upon ever new horizons – new lands, new oceans, new continents, new peoples – and even the stay-at-home was awed to silence, as upon a peak in Darien, at the wonder of it all.

Such are some of the considerations necessary to full appreciation of *The Lusiads* against the background of the age which produced it. Yet it would be a major disservice to poem and reader alike to convey, however faintly, the impression that this is something out of a long past world which only so can be re-invested with interest today. The present version springs from the conviction that the poem lives, and deserves to live, if only as a magnificent narrative – based strictly on fact, bearing on every page the authentic touch of one who has himself lived intensely all he writes of, suffused withal with a poet's imagination – of one of the most impressive chapters in the record of human endeavour. High vision, high courage and high adventure have rarely been more admirably compounded; and for so long as these qualities still command our esteem, and this country and her oldest ally continue to sail together those eastern seas 'nunca dantes navegados', *The Lusiads* is unlikely to fail in its appeal to the English reader.

Canto 1. The poet's theme: the glorious achievements of the Portuguese. Invocation to the Muses and dedication to King Sebastião. The gods meet in council on Olympus, Bacchus opposing the Portuguese, Venus and Mars taking their side. Jupiter is well-disposed. Vasco da Gama's vessels are discovered sailing up the east coast of Africa. They touch at Mozambique and have a narrow escape from Moslem treachery, instigated by Bacchus. Arrival at Mombasa. The poet reflects on the uncertainty of life.

Canto 2. Bacchus again plans their destruction at Mombasa. Venus with the Nereids staves off the immediate danger, then hastens to intercede with Jupiter, who foretells the great discoveries and victories reserved to Portugal in the East. He sends Mercury down to prepare a friendly reception for the mariners at Malindi. Da Gama's arrival there. The King of Malindi visits the ships and asks da Gama for information concerning his country and the voyage thither.

Canto 3. Invocation to the Epic Muse. Geographical description of Europe. Lusus, the mythical founder of Lusitania. The political emergence of Portugal. Afonso Henriques, its first king, and the onward sweep of the Reconquest. Brief narrative of succeeding kings and their conquests. The tragic story of Inês de Castro. Fernando I, a weak and unprincipled monarch, endangers his country's independence. The poet reflects on the power of love.

Canto 4. Disturbances on Fernando's death and the threat from Castile. Nuno Alvares rallies the faint-hearts. Description of the battle of Aljubarrota. João I takes Ceuta in Portugal's first overseas enterprise. Further conquests in North Africa by Afonso V and his war against Castile. João II dispatches Covilhã to India by way of the Mediterranean. Appearance to Manoel I in a dream of the Rivers Ganges and Indus. He despatches da Gama in search of India by the Cape. The departure from Lisbon. An old man on the water-front voices the general apprehension and inveighs against ambition.

Canto 5. Narrative of the voyage as far as Malindi. The earlier discoveries. New natural phenomena: the Southern Cross, St Elmo's Fire, the waterspout. Fernão Veloso's adventure among the natives. The giant Adamastor -predicts disaster for subsequent expeditions. His love for Tethys and transformation into the Cape. Fearsome outbreak of scurvy among the crews. Stages of the further journey to Malindi. Da Gama's pride in an achievement without parallel among the ancients, and his hearers' emotion at the recital. The poet reflects on the indebtedness of heroes to poetry for the perpetuation of their fame.

Canto 6. Regal entertainment by the King of Malindi, who also supplies a pilot. The fleet sets sail at length across the Indian Ocean. Bacchus descends to Neptune's under-water court to kindle hatred of the Portuguese, and Aeolus is bidden loose the winds against them. Veloso's tale of the Twelve of England. A violent storm breaks and the vessels all but perish. Da Gama's prayer for deliverance. Venus intervenes with her nymphs and pacifies the winds. With daybreak land is sighted: India at last. The poet reflects on the nature of true heroism.

Canto 7. Praise of the Portuguese for their services to the faith and indictment of Germany, England, France, Italy for disrupting Christendom. First description of India. Da Gama's emissary encounters Monsaide, a Barbary Moslem who speaks Spanish. He comes on board and informs concerning Malabar. Da Gama lands and is taken to the Samorin, to whom he proposes a treaty of friendship. The Catual of Calicut, informed by Monsaide regarding the Portuguese, visits the fleet and sees depicted on banners heroic scenes from Portuguese history. The poet, invoking the nymphs of the Tagus and the Mondego to help him describe them, reflects on his misfortunes, condemns unworthy rulers, and vows to give praise only where praise is due.

Canto 8. Description of the banners, being a review of national heroes from Lusus and Ulysses to Henrique the Navigator. Further reflections on fame and greatness. The Samorin's soothsayers poison his mind against the Portuguese and Bacchus intrigues again with the Moslems, who plot their destruction. Da Gama dispels the Samorin's suspicions and is given leave to bring his merchandise ashore. The Catual detains da Gama, who begins to suspect treachery. He at length secures his freedom in exchange for a share in the merchandise and rejoins his ship. The poet reflects on the power of money.

Canto 9. Two Portuguese factors are held on shore. The Mecca fleet: Monsaide warns da Gama of his peril. He seizes Moslem merchants as hostages, exchanges them for his factors, and weighs anchor, with some natives and samples of spices on board. Venus devises an Island of Love as reward for the mariners, and invokes Cupid's aid. Cupid's punitive measures against mankind for its obstinacy in bestowing love on the wrong objects. Tethys and her Nereids, smitten with love of the mariners, are guided to the island and instructed in their role. Arrival of the vessels. Description of the island's delights and of the chase and capture of the nymphs. Tethys declares herself to da Gama. The poet reveals the symbolic significance of the island.

Canto 10. The banquet of Nereids and mariners. A nymph prophesies the exploits of da Gama's successors in India. Tethys leads da Gama to a mountain-top and there explains to him the structure of the universe, with the earth at the centre of the spheres. Description of the mainland and islands of Africa, Asia and Oceania as discovered or still to be discovered by the Portuguese, with a glance at Brazil. Return of the fleet to Portugal. The poet reflects on the decline of the heroic temper at home, exhorts Sebastião to a deeper regard for those who serve him overseas, and bids him encourage only true worth and take counsel only from experience.

THE TRANSLATION

Few writers illustrate better than Camoens the essential dilemma that confronts the translator in every age. Loyalty to one's author is one thing, loyalty to one's public is another, and the greater the gulf between author and public the greater the conflict. That Camoens has something to say to twentieth-century England as well as to sixteenth-century Portugal will scarcely be denied; but what he has to say can doubtfully be the same in both cases, while of the impossibility of saying it in the same way there can be no doubt whatever.

As much has been made abundantly, if unwittingly, clear by the half-dozen and more who have already attempted the task, from Fanshawe in 1655 to Burton in 1870. They have essayed it in the same *ottava rima* that Camoens took over from Ariosto, in rhyming couplets, in blank verse, in the Spenserian stanza, always in verse. Within this initial fidelity, however relative, to the form of the original, only Mickle (1776) is bold to bear the interests of his prospective readers equally and always in view. It is an over-boldness. Interpreting *The Lusiads* as 'the epic poem of the birth of commerce, and, in a particular manner, the epic poem of whatever country has the control and possession of the commerce of India', he virtually takes it over as something thrown in with that empire of the East to which England had in his day succeeded, and thinks nothing of interpolating a 300-line naval engagement of his own imagining or of cutting by two-thirds Camoens' moving peroration. Others, if not always proof against what Burton called 'the prurience of respectability', eschewed Mickle's temptation by seeking deliberately to give a tone of antiquity to their versions.

Here Burton himself went to the extreme, and the result is a classic example of how an exclusive fidelity to one's author may defeat the whole purpose of translation. His object was to provide such a poem as Camoens might have written had he been born instead an Englishman, although the attempt to write Elizabethan English in the nineteenth century already overlooked the detail that no readers of that age had survived. Nor was this all, for in a vain effort to convey further the impression of sixteenth-century Portuguese he clogged his style with hyperbaton, syncope, apocope, aphaeresis, diaeresis, paragoge. The interests of the modern English reader were nowhere consulted, and the upshot was as could have been foreseen: his version, the most ambitious of all and the most firmly rooted in scholarship, fell from the press stillborn, unreadable.

The present translation is believed to be the first ever made into English prose. It aims at rendering a service to the living, not pious tribute to the dead, and is concerned therefore with the substance, not the form, of the original. This is not disrespect to a great poet. Grievous as were the shifts to which fidelity in form reduced those who sought to render *Os Lusíadas* into the same intricate stanza pattern as the original, forgetful that no two languages agree in their resources of expression, still less in the syllable-count of given words or phrases or in the facility and abundance of rhyme, it should be remembered further that the greatest poet must nod or falter not once but many a time in a poem of over a thousand eight-line stanzas. The abuse of epithet and adverb, the lapse into tag and padding, the sheer prose of many a weary mechanical solution to the ever-recurring problem, in a historical-geographical narrative, of versifying the essentially prosaic, these defects, that are nowhere found in Camoens the lyric poet, are chargeable not to him but to his medium.

That medium still allowed a substantial measure of sustained felicity in many an unforgettable passage and word-picture. In general the author's poetic inspiration soars in proportion as theme or sentiment approaches the lyrical: witness the passages that treat of Inês de Castro, Aljubarrota, the old man on the water-front at Lisbon, Adamastor, Venus interceding with Jupiter, the Island of Love. But the penalties the verse-form imposes in translation absolve from servile respect for it as sacrosanct to the detriment of all else.

Another adjustment here made in favour of the modern reader calls for a word of explanation. Poetry, like prose, is in every age an art of communication. The two differ in that the language of poetic communication, while never independent of dictionary values, is charged also with associations deriving from the whole cultural heritage to which the poet is heir; and his readers, the public to whom he consciously addresses himself, will be those who share that heritage and respond to those associations. The heritage of the English poet today is the corpus of English poetry down the ages, with all that this may have absorbed of the poetry of other nations.

The heritage to Camoens, as to his time, meant Greece and Rome. In their poetry he was steeped, from them he had learnt all he knew of the nature and procedures of poetry, of its language and technique, its resources for the procuring of specific effects, its themes. To them he turned for simile and metaphor, from them he borrowed unblushingly whatever his own language lacked. In particular he adopted, as his happy hunting-ground of fancy and the imagination, the whole world of classical mythology.

The significance of this in the general framework, the 'machinery', of the poem has been seen already. Its other implication is this, that who would read *Os Lusíadas* as it stands must be no less conversant than was Camoens with that world of myth and fable. For the vast majority of the Portuguese of his day, who had not received a humanistic education, a large part of his masterpiece would have been scarcely less intelligible written in Greek. Camoens had himself asked his friend do Couto to supply a commentary on the work, and rare indeed are editions for the Portuguese reader that have presumed to dispense with such. That of Faria e Sousa (1639) is perhaps excessive: it runs, with the text, to 2,396 pages. Few fail at least to equal the poem in length. Burton's commentary to his English translation filled two volumes.

Once it be realized, however, that this difficulty is inherent neither in the story nor in the thought, but only in a convention of poetic allusion that was the fashion of an age now dead and gone, the path of the translator who would give the work a new lease of life is clear. He must translate not merely from Portuguese into English, but from the idiom of the sixteenth into that of the twentieth century.

> 'Twas the glad season when the God of Day
> into Europa's rav'sher 'gan return;
> when warmèd either point his genial ray
> and Flora scatter'd Amalthéa's horn.

So Camoens, literally rendered by Burton. What he means is: 'It was early April, the season when flowers abound.' Or again:

> 'Twas in the season when th' Eternal Light
> entered the Beast that workt Nemaea's woe;

meaning simply the month of July. By 'the god who in Amphion-ean Thebae rose' the reader is expected to understand Bacchus; by 'the glowing Amourist who won fair faithless Larissaea's love', Apollo. 'Jove's valiant bird' is the eagle, 'the bird whose song the Phaëtonian death wailed loud and long', the swan; the inhabitants of the torrid zone appear as 'they who dwell beneath the Ram'. Venus is now Cytherea, now Erycina, now Dione, now the Cyprian goddess, now the Paphian. It is in short a mark of erudition – and Renaissance poets were much concerned to show how learned they were – to refer to the gods and heroes of antiquity by allusion or association rather than directly, so showing how much at home the writer felt in the world of Virgil and Ovid.

For such learning the modern term is pedantry, and it becomes an elementary service to the reader of today, and no disservice to Camoens at this remove in time, to call things by their names and to ask of each divinity that he or she be content with one. The reader will judge whether, this being done, the work has gained or lost in his esteem. The only other liberty knowingly taken concerns the use and abuse of epithet. Some of these, like 'fierce', 'proud', 'valiant', are sadly overworked throughout, and on occasions where they serve at most to fill out the line, adding nothing to sense or suggestion, to omit has appeared to fall within a prosifier's discretion.

The handling of Portuguese names in translation is a problem of a different nature. If some – the Ferdinands, Peters, and Sebastians – have their English equivalent, and others – a Henry the Naviga-tor or a Magellan the Circumnavigator – are long acclimatized in

34

our historical literature, the greater part remain obstinately Portuguese and will not be Englished. As between the lesser incongruity of retaining João, Estêvão, Duarte in an English text and the greater of sowing confusion in this goodly company of Lusitanians – Egas Moniz, Nuno Alvares, Gonçalo Ribeiro, Vasco da Gama, Afonso de Albuquerque, the Sequeiras, da Cunhas, Sampaios and their peers – with an occasional discordant John, Stephen or Edward, the choice has been easy. Nor need pronunciation be an obstacle to readers who would savour this beadroll on the tongue if it be remembered that the tilde (~) over a vowel denotes nasalization, while *nh*, *lh* are single palatal consonants roughly equivalent to *ny*, *lli* in English 'canyon', 'million'.

It should be added that Portuguese orthography was far from settled in Camoens' time — in some respects it is not settled yet – and that names appear spelt in the original in two or three different ways. The forms given in the translation are accordingly those of modern usage. Occasional Spanish names also occur in the narrative, but add no complication, save perhaps on one occasion where Spanish Alfonso and Portuguese Afonso, meeting as allies on a Spanish battle-field, will be found referred to as 'the two Alfonsos'.

Geographical names are in different case. Where anglicized forms of foreign place-names are as firmly rooted in usage as are Lisbon and Oporto they become an essential element in recognition, and 'Lisboa', 'Porto' must yield or be charged with affectation. The majority of the places mentioned in *The Lusiads* lie, moreover, far outside Portugal, while some are no longer known by the names there given. They have therefore been rendered throughout, when identifiable, by the forms current in modern English. The term 'Moor', that Camoens uses as a synonym for 'Moslem', has been retained only when the reference is to Morocco.

The reader will bear in mind, finally, that no major work of literature written close on four hundred years ago in any language, our own included, lies open to our full comprehension today. In Camoens, as in Shakespeare, there are points of interpretation, as of textual reading, over which the most authoritative scholars may still disagree. It is a translator's duty in such cases to make up his mind; and any who, confronting this version with the Portuguese text, feel moved to dissent from the solution proffered in a particular crux may accept at least that the alternatives were long and carefully weighed in the light of the evidence. More rarely, as in the matter of the famous two sieges of Diu of 1538 and 1545, the high-water mark not only of Portuguese bravery and tenacity in the East but of the East's desperate attempts to re-master its own, difficulty resides not in interpretation but in an over-elliptical style which takes certain historical knowledge for granted, or even in plain oversight on the poet's part; and here, in some few passages, the going has been eased for the reader lacking that knowledge by discreet interpolation, denoted by square brackets.

The translator has sought throughout to square his conscience with both loyalties. Where there was no striking an exact balance between them he has been content that the pointer should incline rather in favour of the reader, since it is for him the translation was made. To offer *The Lusiads*, in any tongue, in a plain text unencumbered by a single footnote, that he who runs may read, is in itself no slight novelty.

W. C. A.

Bearsden, February 1950

THE LUSIADS

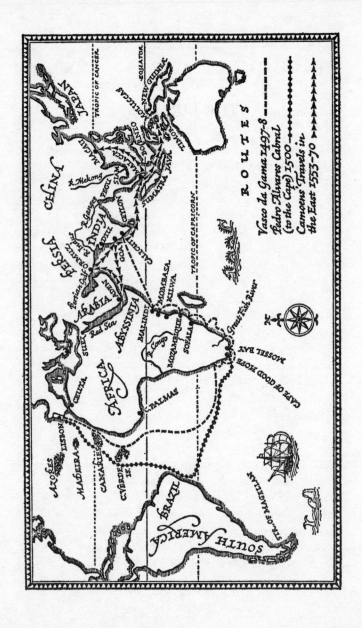

ROUTES

Vasco da Gama 1497–8 ▪▪▪▪▪▪
Pedro Alvares Cabral
(to the Cape) 1500 ●●●●●●
Camoens' Travels in
the East 1553–70 »»»»»»

CANTO

I

THIS is the story of heroes who, leaving their native Portugal behind them, opened a way to Ceylon, and further, across seas no man had ever sailed before. They were men of no ordinary stature, equally at home in war and in dangers of every kind: they founded a new kingdom among distant peoples, and made it great. It is the story too of a line of kings who kept ever advancing the boundaries of faith and empire, spreading havoc among the infidels of Africa and Asia and achieving immortality through their illustrious exploits. If my inspiration but prove equal to the task, all men shall know of them.

Let us hear no more then of Ulysses and Aeneas and their long journeyings, no more of Alexander and Trajan and their famous victories. My theme is the daring and renown of the Portuguese, to whom Neptune and Mars alike give homage. The heroes and the poets of old have had their day; another and loftier conception of valour has arisen.

Nymphs of the Tagus, you have inspired in me a new and burning zeal. To your stream I have always paid glad tribute in my humble verse. Grant me now nobler, sublimer strains, a style at once grandiloquent and flowing, that Apollo may recognize in your waters another fountain of the Muses. Give me the grand, resounding fury, not of rustic pipe or flute, but of the trump of war that fires men's breasts and brings a flush to the cheek. Give me a song equal to the deeds of your so warlike people, a song destined to be known and sung throughout the world, if indeed a poet may achieve so much.

I address you too, Sebastião, noble scion and guaranty of the ancient liberties of Portugal and no less certain hope of increase to this small corner of Christendom, pride and portent of our age, sent by God to strike new terror into Moslem hearts and to win for the faith vast new regions of the earth. You are sprung from a royal line more dear to God than any other in the West, even though it may not be styled 'Imperial' or 'Most Christian': the proof is in your coat-of-arms, recalling his appearance on the victorious field of Ourique, when he bestowed as your country's escutcheon the five wounds he suffered on the cross.

Great King, whose far-flung dominions greet the sun's gaze alike when it rises, when half-way through its course, and when it sinks to rest, at whose hands we look to see Arab, Turk, and Indian shamed and humbled: lay aside for a spell the majesty that will not be read more clearly in your countenance when, in the fulness of time, eternity shall claim you than it may now; deign, with royal magnanimity, to cast your eyes earthwards and behold one more token of affection for the valorous deeds of our native land, here told in melodious numbers.

In them you will find, too, love of this our country itself, an emotion stirred by the hope not of base recompense but of a noble, perhaps eternal, reward; for it is no small thing to be known as one who exalted the land that gave him birth. Give ear then, while I sing the greatness of the race that acknowledges your sway, and judge thereafter which is the more excellent, to be master of the whole world or to rule over such a people.

There will be no pursuit here of mere national aggrandizement, no praising with false attributions, flights of fancy and feats of the imagination, as is the Muse's wont in other lands. The deeds I tell of are real, and far outstrip the fabled adventures of any Rodamonte, Ruggiero or Orlando, even granting that Orlando did exist. In place of these you will meet a valiant Nuno Alvares, who did such notable service to his king and country,

*an Egas Moniz, a Fuas Roupinho, for whom alone I wish I had
the lyre of Homer. The twelve knights Magriço led to England
are more than a match for the paladins of France, the illustrious
Vasco da Gama for Aeneas himself.*

*Should you seek an equal in fame to Julius Caesar or Charle-
magne, consider Afonso I, whose lance may cast into the shade
any foreign reputation; or João I, who on the glorious field of
Aljubarrota assured his country's independence; or João II, an-
other invincible warrior; or Afonsos III, IV, and V. Nor shall
those be forgotten who, fighting beneath your ever-victorious
banner, have scaled such heights in the lands of the rising sun:
most valiant Pacheco, the dread Almeidas whose loss the Tagus
still mourns, Albuquerque the terrible, stout Castro, and many
another who has triumphed over death itself.*

*While I sing of these – of you, most noble King, I cannot, for
I dare not – you are assuming the reins of government and will in
due course give matter for such a poem as has never yet been
heard. Let Africa and the seas beyond begin to feel the weight
of your armies and their exploits, until the whole world tremble.
The Moslem fixes his eye on you in terror, recognizing the
symbol of his destruction; the barbarous heathen at sight of you
bends his neck to the yoke. Tethys, wife of the sea-god, offers
you one of her nymphs as bride, so enamoured is she of your
youth and comeliness, and the whole realm of ocean as dowry;
while, looking down from their Olympian abode, your grand-
fathers João III and Carlos V, one famous in peace as the other
in war, see themselves again in you and look to you to renew
their memory and their deeds of valour. And there beside them,
in the temple of eternity, your place is already reserved.*

*But first a long reign awaits you: it is your people's will. And
meantime pray bestow your favour on this bold enterprise, that
these verses of mine may be yours too. Look on your Argonauts
as they plough the angry waves, and let them know that your*

eye is upon them. Be prepared to hear them often invoke your
name.

Vasco da Gama and his men were already sailing across
the restless ocean. The winds blew softly, filling their sails.
Only the seals disputed their passage. The waters were
flecked with foam.

Up on Olympus, the gods were assembling in council
to consider future happenings in the East. Jupiter had sent
his summons out by Mercury, and now, from north, south,
east and west, down the Milky Way they came, treading
the crystal skies, leaving to their own devices all the seven
spheres entrusted to them by the Supreme Power who
governs heaven, earth, and angry sea by thought alone.

There, on his starry throne, sat in sublime state the father
of them all, the god of the thunderbolt, noble, stern,
majestic, his countenance irradiating such an air of the
divine as might confer on mortals immortality, his crown
and glittering sceptre of a stone that outsparkled the dia-
mond. On lesser but still resplendent thrones, inlaid with
gold and pearls, sat the other gods each according to his
rank, the older and more venerable enjoying their due
precedence. And now Jupiter spoke, in a grave and awe-
some voice:

'Eternal dwellers in the starry heavens, you will not have
forgotten the great valour of that brave people the Portu-
guese. You cannot therefore be unaware that it is the fixed
resolve of destiny that before their achievements those of
Assyrians, Persians, Greeks and Romans shall fade into
oblivion. Already with negligible forces – you were wit-
nesses – they have expelled the Moslem, for all his strength
and numbers, from the entire region of the Tagus; while
against the redoubtable Castilians they have invariably had

heaven on their side. Always, in a word, they have known victory in battle and have reaped, with its trophies, fame and glory too.

'I need not dwell on their renown of old when, led by Viriato, they covered themselves with glory in the struggle against Rome; nor on the memory they left behind them when they fought under their chosen leader Sertorius, the same who, not being one of them, feigned to derive his authority from a divinely-inspired doe.

'Now you see them bold to dare still more, scorning the tempests and other hazards of the deep and embarking on frail vessels for goals whither none till now has ever ventured. For some time past they have been sailing through temperate climes, where the length of the day varies with the seasons, and now they are altering course and have set themselves to discover the sun's very cradle in the East. Fate has promised them – and its decrees are irrevocable – that they shall for long be supreme on this ocean which sees it rise.

'They have now passed a severe winter at sea, which has reduced them to dire straits, and deserve to have the new lands they seek revealed to them. Seeing therefore that their voyage has been so beset with perils and buffetings, with tempestuous headwinds and extremes of climate and of weather, I have resolved that on the farther coast of Africa they shall now find a friendly welcome and the opportunity to refit their wearied fleet before setting out once more on their long journey.'

Jupiter had spoken, and the other gods now raised their voices in discussion, some approving, others opposing his decision. Among the latter was Bacchus, who knew that if the Portuguese were to reach the East his own exploits there would be forgotten. He was already aware of the prophecy that a redoubtable Iberian race should cross over the seas to India and subjugate its coastal regions, and that their victories should overshadow all those of which history told, whether his or another's; it grieved him sorely to think of losing a repute of which Nysa, his own foundation there, still kept the memory green. So far neither fortune nor circumstance had ever deprived him of his eminence as the one who overran the lands of the Indus: the poets were there to prove it. If now the Portuguese were to get so far, the dark waters of Lethe, he had good cause to fear, would engulf his name and fame.

Venus felt differently. She was attracted to the Portuguese, seeing in them many of the qualities of the ancient Rome she had loved so much: their stout hearts and favouring fortune – witness the conquests in North Africa – their tongue, which may so easily be taken for a Latin once removed. And there was another reason. The Fates had given her clearly to understand that, wherever this warlike race extended its sway, there too her praises would be sung.

And so the two contended, the god moved by the dread of waning prestige, the goddess by the hope of new honours to come. Neither would give way, and the friends of each rallied to his or her support. When the winds rage fiercely through the dark forest, leaving a trail of devastation in their wake, the whole countryside clamours and re-echoes with the commotion: such was the tumult that broke out among the gods gathered on Olympus.

But now Mars stood up. He was the most forthright in taking Venus's side, either remembering his love for her of old or because the Portuguese deserved no less. There was anger in his glance as he threw back the heavy shield that hung from his neck and raised somewhat the visor of his diamond helmet. He made an impressive figure as he

44

took his stand firmly before Jupiter, determined to voice his opinion; and when he struck the throne a resounding blow with his cudgel the very heavens trembled and the sun, taken aback, shone for a moment with an uncertain light. He spoke:

'Father of the gods, all creation is your handiwork and owns your sway. You cannot wish this race, whose virtues and achievements have won your profound esteem, and which now seeks to discover a new hemisphere, to suffer ignominy. Your decision was taken long since. As an upright judge, do not listen any longer to interested and suspect pleadings. If reason were not here a prey to excess of fear, it would be more fitting that Bacchus should uphold the Portuguese, since it is from his boon companion Lusus that they derive their other name of Lusitanians.

'But enough of his hostility: it is base-born, of spleen, and envy is powerless against the good that others deserve and heaven has willed. Do not go back, great Jupiter, on your resolve; to put your hand to something and then desist is weakness. Mercury is swifter than wind or arrow. Dispatch him forthwith to guide the mariners ashore at some spot where they may refit and inform themselves concerning India.'

Jupiter nodded his agreement to Mars' demands. He then sprinkled nectar over the assembled gods and each, making due obeisance, departed back along the Milky Way to his own abode.

While this scene was taking place on Olympus, the Portuguese sailed on and on. They had rounded the Cape now and were heading north again between the mainland and the island of Madagascar. The sun beat down pitilessly; the season was early spring. The winds wafted them gently along – was not heaven their friend? – under a serene and cloudless sky. No thought of danger crossed their minds.

As they left Cape Corrientes behind more islands came into view. To Vasco da Gama, their stalwart leader – and a right proper man he was for such an enterprise, proud and indomitable of heart, always smiled on by fortune – there was no cause here to break their journey. The islands appeared to be deserted and he decided to continue on his course. But the matter turned out otherwise.

For straightway, from the one that seemingly lay nearest to the mainland, there put out several small craft with long sails, which made swiftly towards them. The Portuguese were greatly excited, and with keen expectation began asking what this could portend. 'Of what race can these people be?' they said to one another. 'What will their customs be like? And their religion? And whose subjects are they?'

The canoes were long, narrow, and very fast, with sails made of palm-leaves woven like mats. Those who manned them were of burnt complexion and wore cotton loin- and shouldercloths, some white, some striped in various colours, and light caps. The shouldercloths they now tucked jauntily under their arms. For the rest they were naked. As weapons they had daggers and short swords; and as they approached they blew on long trumpets.

Waving their arms and cloths, they made signs to the vessels to await them. The Portuguese were already turning their prows to run in under the islands, every man lending a hand as if the end of their labours were in sight. Soon the sails were furled, the upper yards struck, and the anchors were thrown overboard with a loud splash.

They were scarcely at anchor before the islanders were clambering up the ropes. Their expression was cheerful, and the Captain gave them a friendly reception, ordering tables to be spread and glasses filled. They drank the wine without hesitation, and, eating merrily, enquired in Arabic who the strangers were, from what land and over what seas they had come, and what they sought.

The others replied: 'We are Portuguese from the West: we seek the lands of the East. We have sailed the seas that reach from the North to the South Pole, skirting the length of Africa and nodding acquaintance with many a land and sky. We are subjects of a powerful king, so esteemed and beloved by everyone that in his service we would gladly brave not merely the broad ocean but the very waters of the under-world. It is at his command we have sailed into the unknown, with only the ungainly seals for company, and seek those eastern lands where the Indus flows. And now,' they ended, 'it is only fair that you tell us, truthfully, of what race you are and what land this is you dwell in. Tell us too whether you know anything of India.'

One of the islanders spoke for the rest. 'We are foreigners here, too, and have nothing in common with the natives. They are pagans, and uncivilized. We are Moslems of the true faith, like the rest of the world. This small island where we live is called Mozambique, and is a port of call for all shipping up and down the coast, whether from Kilwa, Mombasa or Sofala. That is why we have settled here. And seeing that you have come so far, and are bound for India, you will have need of a pilot. That we can supply, and refreshment. But our Governor will wish to see you. He will look to any further needs you may have.'

With this the Moslem and his fellows took polite leave of da Gama and his men, and returned to their canoes. The sun was setting.

That night a strange and unlooked-for joyousness took

possession of the weary crews, at having word at long last of the far land. The men fell to reflecting on their visitors and their odd ways, marvelling that the followers of Islam should have spread to such distant parts. By now the moon was shining bright, its beams shimmering on the silvery waters. The heavens were specked with stars like daisies on a meadow. In their dark lairs the raging winds lay at rest. Watch on board was mounted as usual.

At length dawn shook out her tresses and a red sunrise announced a new day. The sailors set about decking out their vessels and running up bright awnings, that the Governor of the islands might be received with proper festivity. He had already put off to visit the Portuguese, bringing with him a gift of food, and imagining to himself that the newcomers must be Turks, of that same barbarous race that from its home by the Caspian had set out to conquer Asia and had already been allowed by fate to overrun the Byzantine Empire.

Da Gama welcomed the visitor and his company with open arms, and made him a present of preserves and wine and rich cloths, of those he had brought from Portugal for just such occasions. The Moslem accepted it all gladly, and ate and drank more gladly still. The mariners meantime, intrigued by the strangers' behaviour and by the corrupt and barbarous Arabic they spoke, had climbed the rigging the better to watch the scene.

The Governor was an intelligent man, but he was puzzled as his eye took in the newcomers' dress and complexion and the strength of their fleet. At length he asked whether by chance they hailed from Turkey, and wished to see the books of their faith that he might know if they too were Mohammedans or, as he now suspected, Christians. Finally, to satisfy his curiosity to the full, he desired they would show him the weapons with which they engaged in battle.

'I shall gladly give you an account of myself, my religion and my arms,' da Gama answered through an interpreter. 'We are not from Turkey, and have no dealings with that troublesome race. We come from Europe, the home of strong and warlike peoples, and are bound for India. Our religion is that of the true God, Creator and Lord of the universe, who suffered scorn and dishonour for our sakes and, having undergone a cruel and unjust death, came back to earth that he might raise mankind to be with him in heaven. The books you ask of me concerning this great and infinite God who became man I have not with me, having no need to carry on paper what is written in my soul. Your desire to see our weapons, that I can satisfy. Examine them as a friend: I warrant you will never wish to see them as an enemy.'

He bade his men show their armament: coats of armour, gleaming breastplates both solid and laminated, fine mail, shields of divers designs, cannon-shot, muskets of pure steel, longbows with their quivers full of arrows, sharp halberds, trusty pikes. Then they brought out the fire-bombs, sulphur-pots, and mortars, though da Gama would not have his men fire these off, for it is no part of breeding or valour to make a display of might before a few timorous strangers. To play the lion among sheep is a puny role.

The Moslem observed everything with keen interest. He had already conceived something much stronger than ill-will towards the new arrivals. But of this his smiling face and much pretence of pleasure showed nothing. Until such time as the designs he was now harbouring were ripe he would treat them affably.

And now the Captain asked him for pilots, promising to

any who would conduct him to India a handsome reward for their pains. The other undertook that he should have them; but there was poison in his heart as he spoke. He wished it had been in his power, not to give them pilots, but to deal them death there and then, so deep was the sudden hatred engendered by the discovery that the Portuguese were Christians. But such are the unfathomable secrets of God, that those who serve him never lack a perfidious enemy.

Eventually, with much feigning of courtesy, and still cheerful, the Moslem took his leave. His canoes soon traversed the narrow stretch of water and deposited him and his men back on their island home.

All this was seen by Bacchus from his abode in the heavens, and when he observed how ill the Moslem had taken the arrival of the Portuguese it occurred to him that he had but to manoeuvre them into a trap to work their final destruction. He mused again over his grievance. 'Fate has decreed that these Portuguese shall win mighty victories over the peoples of India. Am I, the son of Jupiter, and in myself so nobly endowed, to tolerate that another shall be exalted by destiny and my own name eclipsed? Once before, the gods willed that one Alexander should wield power in those regions and by might of arms reduce them to his yoke. But it is not sufferable that this handful of men should be gifted with such skill and daring that alike Alexander and Trajan and I should have to give way to the name of Portugal.

'It shall not be. Before this Captain ever sees India, I will lay such pitfalls for him as shall foil him completely of his purpose. The opportunity has offered, and I am going to seize it. I shall go down to earth and work on the indignation of these Moslems.'

Said and done. Almost beside himself with anger, Bac-
chus came down on African soil, assumed human shape and
features, and set out for the island. The better to weave his
plot, he had taken on the likeness of a wise old Moham-
medan well known in Mozambique and on intimate terms
with the Governor. Choosing a convenient time, he then
called on the latter and informed him that the newcomers
were a thieving lot, for report had already come from the
mainland that, under cover of pacts of friendship, they had
despoiled the coastal tribes wherever they had dropped
anchor.

'I can tell you further,' he said, 'that these bloodthirsty
Christians have been looting and setting fire to practically
every ship they have encountered on the high seas, and that
they have come from a far country with designs already
formed against us. They plan to sack and kill us and to
carry off our wives and children captive.

'I know too that their Captain will be coming ashore
here very shortly for water, with an escort, for a guilty
conscience breeds fear. You take some of your men, armed,
and lie in wait for him. They will be taken off their guard,
and you can easily ambush them. Should you not manage
to account for the lot, I have thought of another stratagem
that may appeal to you. Find them a pilot, but a prudent,
crafty one who can lead them to their doom, whether
through defeat in an engagement, or by taking them off
their course, or drowning, it does not matter.'

The Governor, himself an old hand in such matters,
threw his arms round the other's neck and thanked him
warmly for his counsel. He set his hostile preparations in
train straightway, planning that the water the Portuguese
were in need of should run red with their blood. And, tak-
ing thought too to the second string to his bow, he looked

out a Moslem pilot whom at need he could send to the ships, a wily fellow who was up to any wickedness and one he knew he could rely on. Him he primed to accompany da Gama, should he succeed in escaping alive from the island, and to pilot him to some certain death.

It was morning, and the sun was already high when da Gama decided to go ashore for water. His men were with him, all armed. As they got into the boats one would have said they already knew about the plot. They might well have suspected it, for the heart's intuitions do not lie. Earlier da Gama had sent to the Governor repeating his request for a pilot, and the answer had been couched in surprisingly unfriendly terms. Partly on this account, partly because he knew the danger of placing trust in a faithless adversary, he had taken such precautionary measures as he could before setting out now with all three of his boats for the island.

The Moslems were already scattered about the shore, re-solved to deny him the water he sought. Some were armed with short lance and shield, others with bow and poisoned arrows, waiting for the Portuguese to land. Numbers more lay in ambush, with some few in front of them in the open, to lure the enemy on. As the boats drew near, those on the white sandy beach began making warlike gestures with shield and lance, on purpose to provoke them. The Portu-guese were not men to suffer such dogs to show their teeth, and they leapt on shore so impetuously that none could say who was first.

When the enraptured lover in the arena knows that his fair lady is looking on, he does not wait for the bull to at-tack, but by running to this side and to that, jumping, whistling, shouting and making passes, does all he can to enrage it. At length the fierce animal puts its head down, gives a roar, and charges, its blind rush spelling disablement and possible death to any in its path.

Such was the burst of fire that now thundered from the boats, spreading death all around and making the air echo with the report. The Moslems' courage broke, panic chilled their blood. The timorous came out from their cover and fled; those who had been so rash as to show themselves died.

The Portuguese followed up the victory with more killing and destruction; for the settlement had no walls or other defences, and under bombardment its dwellings collapsed and burst into flames. The Governor had good cause now to regret the skirmish: he had looked for an easier issue. The old and helpless, the mother with the child at her breast, might be heard cursing all war.

The Moslems shot their arrows as they fled, but they were too frightened and in too great a hurry to shoot to any effect. They hurled pebbles, sticks, large stones and whatever else came to hand in their mad fury. Then, abandoning everything and turning their backs on the island, they made panic-stricken for the sea and struck out for the mainland but a short distance away. Those who could crowded into canoes, on which the Portuguese rained shot, smashing many to pieces. The rest swam, some only to be engulfed by the waves and perish, others, swallowing the sea-water, to be spewed back by the sea. Such was their punishment at the hands of the Portuguese for their malice and treachery.

The victors meantime returned to the ships, laden with the rich spoils of war and free to draw water now at their ease, for there was none to gainsay them.

But if the Moslems had taken a severe beating, their hatred burned fiercer than ever at the thought that it should go unavenged. All their hopes now were pinned on their second subterfuge. The Governor, repentant, asked for peace; and the Portuguese were slow to realize that in the guise of peace it was again war he sent them. For his token of good faith was the promised pilot – the false pilot, with evil in his heart, who was to guide them to their deaths.

Wind and weather were favourable, and the Captain was anxious to continue on his journey to India. He gave the pilot a warm welcome, made diplomatic reply to the Governor, and once more spread his sails to the breeze. The ships sped smoothly along, with an escort of nymphs. The loyal crews were in gentle, cheerful mood.

All unsuspecting of the deceit the pilot was hatching, the Captain talked with him at length about the coast they were sailing along, and about India. The Moslem was busy plotting in his mind on the lines suggested by Bacchus: he was to see to it that they never reached India. But he answered freely all da Gama's questions, describing the land they sought and its harbours; and his hearers accepted what he told them as true, and had no misgivings.

Then he spoke of an island not far off whose inhabitants, he said, had for long been of the Christian faith. So Sinon once imposed on the Trojans concerning the wooden horse. The Captain listened with great interest, and was so heartened at the news that he besought the pilot, with many presents, to guide them thither. This was just what the other wanted, for the people of that island were also, needless to say, Mohammedans, and much more numerous than those of Mozambique; and he imagined that now the fate of the Portuguese was sealed. The island's name was Kilwa; it is not unknown to fame.

Towards it, then, the ships now cheerfully turned their

prows. But Venus, observing them depart from their true course, all unwitting that they were being headed to destruction, was not prepared to see her beloved Portuguese perish on such a desolate strand; and by means of contrary winds she defeated the false pilot's intention.

The Moslem, however, was not to be so easily baulked. Thwarted in one direction, he began forthwith plotting in another. Since the winds were against them, he told da Gama, he suggested that they should make instead for another island nearby where some of the inhabitants were Christians, the others being Mohammedans. In this too he lied, true to his instructions, for there were no Christians there either.

But the Captain still believed all he said, and set his course accordingly. Venus had not ceased to be watchful, and this time she prevented him from crossing the bar, so that he was obliged to cast anchor outside. This island lay so close to the mainland that only a narrow strait divided them. It boasted a city with imposing buildings stretching along the sea-front, and a king, now advanced in years. Island and city alike were called Mombasa. Da Gama felt strangely elated at the thought of finding here a people of Christians.

And now boats put out from the island, bearing a message from its king. He was already informed regarding the newcomers; for Bacchus, repeating his earlier manoeuvre, had long since spoken with him too, in the same Moslem disguise. It was a message ostensibly of peace, but it cloaked a poisonous intent, as the sequel showed only too clearly.

Truly the dangers that beset us as we journey uncertainly through life are many and grievous. To pin one's hopes on another, and find him plotting against one's life! To encounter at sea such constant storms and havoc and peril of death, and find on land no less constant hostility, deception, and refusals to extend a helping hand! Where is frail man to turn for succour? Where may he live out his brief span in safety, secure in the knowledge that the heavens will not vent their indignation on so insignificant an insect?

THE sun was drawing a curtain over the heavens and sink-ing slowly to rest in Erebus's secret mansions in the waters when the emissaries of deceit reached the vessels, that had scarcely more than cast anchor. Their spokesman, charged with the plot, addressed da Gama:

'Great Captain, the king of this island is overjoyed at your arrival from across the ocean. Your fame has come before you, and so keen is his pleasure that his whole desire is but to know and serve you, and to provide you with whatever you may need. He bids you therefore cross the bar with full confidence; and, since your men must be wearied with the rigours of the voyage, he invites you to heed the promptings of nature and let them rest for a spell on land.

'If it should be the wealth and merchandise of the East you seek, cinnamon, cloves and other burning spices, medi-cinal drugs, glistening rubies and diamonds, here you may find everything in such plenty that you need go no further.'

Da Gama thanked him for the king's message, and ex-plained that as it was getting dark he would not accept the invitation to enter the harbour straightway. In the morn-ing, when he could sail in without risk to his ships, he would gladly comply, if only out of deference to such a ruler. He then enquired whether he had been correctly informed by the pilot that there were Christians on the island. The astute messenger was prepared for this, and told him that the majority of the people were of that faith. With this any misgivings the Captain might have felt were allayed, and he accepted at their face value the protestations of these treacherous unbelievers.

Among his crews were men who, having been condemned at home for crimes, had been assigned to him for any particularly hazardous occasion that might arise. Of these he detailed two, the most resourceful and experienced, to visit the city and gauge its strength, and to make contact with the Christians he so longed to see. By them he sent presents to the king, thinking thereby to make more secure, and if possible even more sincere, the goodwill he proffered, little dreaming that the truth was exactly the opposite. And now the perfidious visitors took leave of the ships and returned to the island, where da Gama's men were given an apparently cordial reception.

Having conveyed to the king their Captain's message and delivered the presents, they went through the city, but were able to see much less than they had hoped. For the cautious Moslems were on their guard, and were not revealing anything. With malice always goes the fear that credits others with harbouring malice too.

Bacchus meantime was still busy with his wiles, all aimed at the mariners' destruction. In a house in the city he had contrived a sumptuous altar, and there, in the garb and semblance now of a Christian, he might have been seen posturing in mock adoration. On the altar was a painting representing the Holy Spirit descending upon the Blessed Virgin in the form of a white dove. Another depicted the company of the apostles, with amazement written on their faces at the gift of languages which had come upon them in tongues of fire.

Here the two men were brought and, kneeling on the ground, they raised their hearts to God, the ruler of mankind. Bacchus burnt sweet incense the while, the false god worshipping the true. Then, welcoming the Christians, he gave them hospitable entertainment for the night, and not once did they suspect how they were being taken in.

With dawn they returned to the ships, assured of the sincerity of the king's friendship. They were attended by the same envoys as before, who came to renew the expression of their master's wish that the ships should now enter the harbour. The two Portuguese told da Gama of their finding holy altars and a saintly priest, and of how they had been entertained and had spent the night. They spoke of having met with nothing but friendliness from king and people alike and all with such frank demonstrations of pleasure at their coming that they were convinced there could be no grounds for apprehension. Da Gama, satisfied now that there was nothing to fear, and that there were Christians on the island, prepared to sail in.

But first he gave a hearty welcome to the Moslems who had returned with them, for the soul too lightly trusts where appearances are so favourable; and they, tying up their craft, swarmed on deck, rejoicing in the thought that the prey was already in their grasp. Those on land were cautiously getting ready arms and ammunition, thinking to rush the ships boldly as soon as they had cast anchor in the river. So, treacherously, they would make an end of the too confiding Portuguese, and settle accounts for the destruction they had wrought at Mozambique.

'Heave ho!' chanted the sailors as they hauled in the anchors, and soon, with foresails only unfurled to the breeze, the ships were gliding slowly towards the buoys that marked the channel.

But Venus had never relaxed her watch over her chosen people. She saw the dread peril that was hidden from them, and like an arrow she sped down to ocean. There she called together the fair sea-nymphs and other deities of the deep – sea-born herself, all were obedient to her command – explained why she had come, and set out with them to head the fleet away from its doom.

The nymphs' silvery tails lashed the waters to foam in their haste. Here Doto might be seen breasting the waves even more impetuously than usual, there Nise leapt and Nerine with a supreme effort skimmed the crests. The billowing waters were alarmed at the Nereids' onrush, and opened a way for them. Venus herself rode furiously on a Triton, her face aflame with anger; her steed, proud to bear so lovely a burden, seemed all unconscious of her weight.

Soon they had caught up with the fleet, its sails now bellying in the fresh breeze. In an instant they had spread out and surrounded the vessels. The goddess with some of her band stationed herself directly in front of the flagship, barring its path to the river-mouth. In vain now did the wind blow and swell the canvas. Placing her gentle breast against the solid prow, she forced the huge vessel back. Others round the sides prized it up and helped push it away from the hostile bar.

When the provident ants, impelled to unwonted effort by fear of the harsh winter ahead, move in cumbrous supplies to the ant-hill, they toil and labour and show a vigour none had believed possible. Such were the strivings now of the nymphs as they sought to avert from the Portuguese the fearsome end that lay in wait for them. The ship was driven back in spite of its crew, who raised angry shouts as they struggled feverishly with the sails and cast the rudder over, now to this side, now to that. From the poop the wary master was shouting orders: he had spotted a sunken rock just ahead and feared it must shiver the vessel's timbers. It was all to no purpose.

The sailors were chanting and shouting so lustily as they toiled and making such a commotion that the Moslems imagined some desperate combat was afoot, and they were filled with terror. Ignorant of the reason of all the turmoil, and not knowing which way to turn in the confusion, the thought struck them that their plot had been discovered and that they were going to be made to pay the penalty forthwith. In a trice they leapt from the ship's sides. Some were able to throw themselves into their canoes and cast off; the others, falling into the water, surfaced and made off swimming. Fear had left them no choice, other than delivering themselves into the hands of the enemy.

In a woodland pool frogs will rashly leave the water on occasion and clamber up the banks. But should they hear anyone approach, the water resounds with the splashes as they leap back and scurry to the safety of their holes, with only their heads visible. Such was the flight of the Moslems, and with them fled, too, plunging into the waves, the pilot who had brought the ships to such a pass, for he likewise feared that his deceit was known. The crew, for its part, was concerned to avoid disaster on the sunken rock, and cast anchor once more; and the other vessels followed suit.

And now da Gama was free at last to consider the so strange and unexpected behaviour of the islanders and, too, the precipitate flight of the pilot. Suddenly the truth of their foul intention dawned on him. And when he took note that it was not from any contrary or blustering winds or adverse current that his ship had been unable to proceed, he held it all supernatural.

'What an amazing experience!' he mused. 'This is beyond question a miracle that has saved us from walking blindly into a trap and has shown up the enmity of these dishonest miscreants. But who can hope of his own wisdom to escape unscathed the evil that men plot, unless the guardian power above come to the succour of human frailty? Divine Providence has made it clear to us that there is scant security to be found in these ports. We have seen only too convincingly how our confidence has been belied.

'Seeing, then, that neither human wisdom nor foresight can avail against such feignings and deceits, I beseech thee, God, to take under thy protection one who, failing thee, must abandon hope. And if pity for this wretched, errant band has so moved thee that, out of thy divine goodness alone, thou hast saved us from the malign and treacherous foe, lead us now, I pray thee, to some haven that is genuinely safe, or reveal to us the land we seek, since it is in thy service alone we sail.'

This pious prayer was heard by Venus, and moved her deeply. Taking leave of the nymphs, who grieved to see her go so soon, she soared again to the starry regions. Her own third heaven welcomed her back, but she did not stop there, but pressed on to the sixth, the seat of Jupiter himself, where she arrived all flushed with the journey, her face radiating such dazzling beauty that the sky and stars above, the air around and all who beheld her were smitten with love of her. From her eyes, where Cupid makes his abode, there flashed a generous warmth that set the icy poles on fire and confused the frigid with the tropic zone.

Jupiter had always loved her dearly. Now, to make him love her still more, she appeared before him as once, in the grove on Mount Ida, she had to Paris. Actaeon the huntsman paid for his glimpse of Diana as she bathed by being changed into a stag. Had he seen Venus now instead, his hungry hounds would never have slain him: desire would have wrought an even speedier death.

Her golden tresses fell carelessly over a neck whiter than snow. As she moved – Cupid waxing sportive unseen – the nipples on her breasts danced. From her gleaming waist shot the flames that set men's hearts on fire, while up her comely limbs the ivy of desire entwined itself. A veil of finest sendal paid due tribute to modesty, neither concealing nor revealing all: its purpose, with the hint of rosy flesh beneath, but to fire longing with redoubled ardour. Already Vulcan her husband was consumed with jealousy, and Mars again with love; and the whole heavens knew it.

Smiles and sadness mingled in her angelic countenance. As a fair lady will laugh and complain in the same breath, showing herself at once merry and annoyed when her too impetuous lover has offended her with his playful attentions, so the peerless goddess spoke to Jupiter, in a tone of cajolery rather than grief:

'I always thought, great Father of the gods, to find you gentle, approachable, loving in matters where my affections were deeply engaged, even though it meant offending someone else. But since I now see you enraged against me, although I have not deserved it nor ever erred in my duty to you, let Bacchus have his way: I shall resign myself to my unhappiness. This people, my people, on whose behalf I shed tears that I see fall in vain – it seems in loving them I have but wrought their hurt, since you are so opposed to my wishes. With sobs and laments I beseech you to succour them, and all my efforts but tell against my own contentment. I love them, and they suffer for it. From now on I will turn my love to hatred, and they will be preserved.

But no: let them perish at the hands of those savage tribes, since I . . .'

And here, pouting, she let fall burning tears that glistened on her face as dew on a fresh rose. For a moment she was silent, as though the words caught in her throat; then, when she would speak again, the Thunderer cut her short. Moved by her gentle tears and protests, that would have softened even a tiger's breast, he smiled on her with that same cheerful visage that, directed downwards, changes the murky sky to a serene radiance. He wiped her tears, then kissed her passionately and threw his arms about her neck. Had they been alone, he would have launched another Cupid there and then.

A child, when caressed by the governess who has just chastised her, will sometimes but weep and sob the more. So Venus as Jupiter pressed her face close to his, until, to calm her angry heart, he began to unfold to her from the secret scrolls of destiny many events that were yet to befall.

'My lovely daughter, have no fear for your Portuguese, nor think that anyone can sway me against those sovereign, tearful eyes of yours. I promise you again, my child, that you shall see Greeks and Romans cast into oblivion by the great deeds this people will perform in the East. Ulysses may have escaped from perpetual captivity on Calypso's island, Antenor have journeyed to the bays of Illyria and to the source of the Timavus, Aeneas have sailed over the angry waters of Scylla and Charybdis. Your people will embark on greater enterprises still, and will discover new worlds to mankind.

'You shall see them build mighty walls, fortresses, cities, see them consistently triumphant over the fierce and belli-cose Turk, see the kings of India, once secure in their inde-pendence, bow the knee to their mighty monarch, until at length they rule supreme and at their hands the peoples receive new and more just laws.

'This Captain who now speeds through the midst of perils in search of the Indus will strike fear and trembling into Neptune himself, until his waves rear independently of the wind, a portent never seen before. What strength and nobility of purpose is theirs who fill the very elements with dread!

'The land that denied them water will yet become a spacious harbour and port of call where vessels sailing from the West will rest a while from their travails. All that coast, but lately plotting deadly pitfalls against them, will accept the yoke and pay tribute, knowing itself powerless against the might of Portugal. The Red Sea will turn yellow with fear. The great kingdom of Ormuz will twice be overrun and subjugated. The Moslem in his hate will find himself transfixed by his own arrows, a warning to all who show hostility to your people that, in resisting, they are but fighting to their own hurt.

'In their defence of Diu through two sieges the Portuguese will show that fortress to be impregnable, will show too by outstanding feats of arms both their calibre and their good fortune. Mars himself will turn envious of their valour and ferocity, and the Moslem will raise a last cry to heaven cursing his false prophet Mahomet.

'Goa will be taken from the infidel, and will come in time to be queen of all the East, raised to a pinnacle by the triumphs of the conquerors; from which proud eminence they will keep the idolatrous heathen, and all such as may be tempted to wage war against your beloved people, severely in check. With an insignificant force they will hold the fortress of Cananor; the large and powerful city of Calicut will be overthrown; in Cochin a proud and outstanding leader will score a victory more deserving of immortality than any ever sung by lyre. All this you shall see come to pass.

'Actium was the scene of a furious clash of arms in the civil wars of Rome when Antony, returning laden with booty from his victories on the Nile, in Bactria and elsewhere in the East – himself a prey to the more lovely than chaste Cleopatra – encountered the fleet of Augustus and was overwhelmed. The waters raged then; but not as they will rage under the trail of conflagration your Portuguese shall leave in their triumphal progress over the nations of Moslems and idolaters. From rich Malacca to distant China and the farthest islands of the East, the whole expanse of ocean shall be subject to them.

'So that, my daughter, even though all peoples everywhere, resenting the challenge, were to exhume their every hero of the past, none to compare with these could they produce. From the Sea of Bengal to the Atlantic, from the waters of the far North to the Strait of Magellan, they will always be peerless, their valour more than human.'

He said no more, but without further delay despatched Mercury to earth to arrange that safe and sheltered harbour where the fleet might put in with confidence. And to ensure that da Gama should not tarry longer in Mombasa, he bade him further reveal to him in a dream the port of refuge ahead.

Mercury donned his helmet, fastened his wings to his feet, and sped down to earth. With him he bore his wand of many uses, whether to close the weary eyes of the dying, call back sad souls from the underworld, or harness the winds. He alighted at Malindi.

Fame had accompanied him, that she might tell the people there of the rare worth of the Portuguese; for an illustrious name of itself constrains to love, and wins its bearer affection and esteem. The natives were thus made friendly in advance, and burned with curiosity to see what manner of men these heroes would turn out to be, and what their demeanour.

From there Mercury continued to Mombasa, where the ships still lay in some apprehension, to warn them to withdraw from that treacherous bar and from a region so little to be trusted. For even skill and valour count for little against the infernal machinations of deceit. Bravery, astuteness, prudence, all rely on friendly guidance from above.

The night was half-spent, and moon and stars shone down brightly on the world. The crews, except for the watch, were asleep. Even the Captain, worn out with his vigil against the hidden perils of the night, was snatching a brief respite.

He dreamt, and in his dream Mercury appeared to him, saying: 'Fly, Portuguese, fly: the wicked king is laying a trap for you, in hopes to destroy you. Fly, now that wind and sky are with you and you have fine weather and a calm sea. Farther on lies the territory of a more friendly ruler where you may find refreshment secure from alarms. Remember the hospitality Diomedes dispensed to those he entertained, feeding their flesh to his horses; remember the infamous Busiris, who would sacrifice his hapless guests on the altar. Such is the fate awaits you here if you delay. Escape while you can from savagery and bad faith.

'Keep to the coast until you come almost to the equator: there you will find this other land I speak of, where the people are true. Their king will give your fleet a warm welcome, he will shower acts of friendship upon you, and finally he will provide you with a reliable pilot to guide you to India.'

With this, Mercury wakened da Gama from his slumber. The Captain sat up with a start, and saw that the shadows of night were shot through with a strange unearthly light. Convinced now of the urgency of getting away from that iniquitous spot, he sent for the master, firm in his new resolve, and bade him spread sail to the wind without a moment's delay. 'It is a command from God,' he explained. 'Heaven is on our side, and has just sent me a special messenger, charged to watch over our footsteps. The breeze is blowing strong: lay on the canvas.'

Soon the sailors were stirring on every hand. They bent to with a will and, chanting, hauled in the anchors. As they did so, they spotted a number of small craft making off in a flurry from under the ships' sides. They were Moslems who had come out under cover of darkness, intending to cut the ships loose so that they would be driven on to the coast and founder. Already they were sawing stealthily at the ropes. But the lynx-eyed Portuguese were one too many for them, and the natives, hearing them on the move again, fled as if their oars had changed to wings.

Once more the sharp prows forged ahead through the silvery waters, riding gently and steadily before the wind. The men's talk was of the dangers that lay behind them; nor were they likely soon to forget the tight places they had found themselves in, and how again and again they had escaped by merest chance with their lives. All that day they sailed.

It was early on the next when they spied two vessels in the distance and, knowing they could only be Moslem, veered in their pursuit. One of the two was taken with panic and sought safety by making for the shore. The other, less resourceful, fell into their hands without a fight, without the firing of a single shot. Its small crew were a craven set and put up no resistance; though if they had they would have fared very much worse.

Da Gama was still vastly desirous of coming by a pilot to show him the route to India, and he reckoned that now at last he had found him. But again it did not turn out as he had hoped, for not one of his captives could even tell him in what direction India lay. They all assured him, however, that at Malindi, not far distant, he could count on finding one. They spoke highly of the king of Malindi, praising his goodness and generosity, his sincerity, magnificence, humanity and other qualities that commanded their deep respect. All this da Gama was able this time to believe, since it tallied with what Mercury had revealed to him in his dream; and he set his course accordingly.

It was early April when the fleet arrived off the kingdom of Malindi, the season when flowers abound, and the sun in its coursings had brought round once again the memory of the resurrection, that set the seal on the life and labours of him to whom all nature owns obeisance. The ships were gay with awnings, and the general gladness bore witness to the men's regard for the sacred day. Banners and standards fluttered in the breeze, the purple clearly visible from afar, and with beating of drums and timbrels they made their festive-martial approach.

The beach was crowded with natives, assembled to see this gay armada. They seemed a trusty, warm-hearted race, very different from those the Portuguese had already encountered. And now the ships stood off-shore, anchors were dropped, and one of the prisoners they had lately taken was sent on land to announce their arrival to the king.

He, already informed of the qualities that so ennobled the Portuguese, set no less store on their having put in at his harbour than their valour deserved; and, speaking from a true and generous heart, he replied entreating them to come ashore and to regard his kingdom as at their service. For once there was no duplicity about the proffered friendship; and with the message he sent a present of sheep, fat poultry and such fruits as were then in season. The gift was generous, the goodwill behind it even more so.

Da Gama gave a joyous welcome to both messenger and message, and sent straightway to the king a present in return, brought on purpose from afar: purple and scarlet cloths, their hues bright as fire, and precious objects of delicately-wrought coral, the substance that grows soft and bush-like under the water and hardens as soon as it is taken out. He sent too as envoy one of his men versed in the language, to exchange with the king formal assurances of peace, and charged him further to convey his excuses for not leaving the ships just at that moment.

The envoy made his way to the king's presence, and addressed him in a style that bespoke the inspiration of Minerva. 'Sublime King,' he said, 'to whom it has been granted from Heaven, by the great dispenser of justice, to sit in authority over a proud and forthright people that fears and loves you equally: know that the strength and security of your harbour are famed throughout all the East. To it and you we have come seeking confidently the help we need. We are no pirates, descending unawares upon defenceless cities to sack and kill by fire and the sword. We hail from the proud continent of Europe, and come sailing in search of the distant regions of India, that great and wealthy land, at the command of our king, a mighty and exalted monarch.

'But what barbarous races there are to be found in the world today, what savagery and bad faith, that will deny to honest men not harbours merely, but the hospitality of the very desert sands! What evil purpose or disposition is it they suspect in us, that they should fear so small a band, and lay snares to destroy us?

'In you, benign ruler, we look on the contrary, and with assurance, to find both loyal friendship and the succour that the shipwrecked Ulysses once received from Alcinous. It was a more than human agent who guided us in safety to this haven; his doing so is proof that in you are to be found a more than common sincerity and goodness of heart.

'And do not think, Your Majesty, that our Captain has been deterred from coming to visit you and to place himself at your service by any discovery or suspicion of double-dealing. In this he but obeys, as ever, the command of his monarch that in no harbour, on no strand, shall he ever leave his ships. You as a king will appreciate that it is the duty of vassals to be governed in all things by their lord, just as the limbs are governed by the head, and would not wish that any should disobey. But he would have you be assured that, as long as rivers shall flow to the sea, so long he and his will remember with gratitude the great favours they now receive at your hand, and will make such return as lies in their power.'

When he had finished, those present all fell to praising the spirit and endurance of men so inured to sea and sky; while the king, dwelling on their solicitous observance of their monarch's injunctions, reflected that he must be a great king indeed who could command obedience at such a distance. The envoy had much impressed him, and, smiling cheerfully, he replied:

'Bid your Captain and his company throw away any evil suspicion or fear they may be harbouring. Their virtues and exploits are such that the world may rightly hold them in high esteem; only the ignoble mind could treat them ill.

As to their not coming ashore to pay me the customary tribute of respect, though I might well take it amiss, still I set great store on obedience in vassals; and if their instructions do not allow them to come, neither should I dream of allowing such loyalty to be tarnished merely to satisfy a desire of mine. Tomorrow morning, at dawn, I shall go out by barge to visit the fleet myself instead. I have been curious to see it for days past. And if, after so long journeyings and such buffetings of wind and sea, it stand in need of re-fitting, here you will find supplies, and munitions, and a pilot you can trust.'

The sun was setting as the messenger returned to the ships bearing this gracious reply. All hearts on hearing it were filled with joy, to think that at last they had the key to the land they sought; and they made the welkin ring with their celebrations. Fireworks rent the air like quivering comets; the thunder of guns struck echoes from sea, land and sky; exploding fire-bombs brought visions of the Cyclops hammering at Vulcan's forge; while the heavens resounded to the strains of lusty song and lustier instrument. Those on shore made reply in kind, letting off rockets that leapt and hissed, Catherine-wheels and flowers of sulphur. Their cries filled the night air. Sea and land alike were lit up as the mimic combat raged to and fro.

But time never stands still, and soon returning dawn sped the last hours of night and summoned mankind to the labours of a new day. The shadows were slowly dissolving from the dew-laden flowers of the field when the king of Malindi embarked to visit the fleet. On the strand there was a great bustling of joyous onlookers. Many were clad in robes of fine purple and richly woven silks. Instead of warlike assegais and bows they carried palm-branches, the true crown of the victor.

A spacious barge, gay with multi-coloured silk awnings, bore the king and his suite of lords and nobles. He came gorgeously attired, after the fashion of the country. On his head he wore a cotton turban, with garnishings of silk and gold. His robe was of fine damask, dyed the Tyrian purple they so highly prized. A collar of fine gold and still finer workmanship encircled his neck. At his belt hung a curiously wrought dagger, the haft glittering with diamonds. His velvet slippers were studded with gold and pearls. An official held aloft a silken umbrella on a long gilt pole to protect him from the burning rays of the sun; while in the prow others drew from bow-shaped trumpets a strange, festive music that was harsh, discordant and even fearsome to the ear.

Da Gama, no less resplendent, put out from the ships to meet his visitor on the water. He too was accompanied in the boats by an honourable and distinguished company. His dress was after the Iberian style, though on top he wore a French cloak of crimson Venetian satin, a colour no less sought after than the Tyrian. The sleeves were caught up with gold buttons that dazzled the eye as they flashed in the sun. His soldier's breeches were embroidered with thread of the same precious metal; so too the delicate ribbons that fastened his doublet. His gold sword he wore after the Italian manner, and in his cap a feather was set at an angle. His followers too struck a pleasing note with their divers attire of purple and other hues that, taken together, vied with the rainbow.

Once more the trumpets sounded, bidding all rejoice. From the beach the natives launched canoe after canoe until the sea was thick with them and their trailing awnings. On the ships the gunners fired their terrifying bombards, that blotted out the sun with their smoke. The shouting rose higher and higher and grew more and more excited, until the Moslems held their hands over their ears.

And now the king had stepped on to da Gama's boat and embraced him, and was received in return with the courtesy due to his rank. Taking in the Captain's every trait and gesture, he showed plainly his astonishment: showed too the profound regard he entertained for men who had come from so far, with so far still to go. In noble terms he again placed his kingdom at the other's service, and bade da Gama but ask for what he needed, for it was already his.

Although, he said, he had never set eyes on any from Portugal before, he knew the nation well by report, for accounts had reached him of their waging war in another land against co-religionists of his. All Africa, in truth, had been full of their prowess when on its soil they won the crown of the kingdom of Mauretania, once the Garden of the Hesperides. He dwelt at length on this, for if it was least among Portugal's titles to fame, it was the greatest that had yet reached his ears.

Da Gama made answer. 'Gracious monarch, you are the first to show kindly feelings towards us Portuguese and to have pity on all the sufferings and adversities that have been our lot on the tempestuous ocean. May God eternal, ruler of Heaven and earth, reward you as we cannot. You alone, in all Africa, have received us with peace after the perils of the deep and given us safe and joyous refuge from the raging winds. While the stars graze on the heavenly pastures, while the sun sheds its light on mankind, and wherever I may be, your praises shall live in men's memories, enshrined in fame and glory.'

The king was still curious to see the fleet, and the boats turned and rowed towards it, encircling each ship in turn to give him the better view. From on board the guns fired a salute of honour and again the trumpets blared, the Moslems replying with their pipes. To the king, who had now seen what he wanted, the bursts of mortar-fire were not merely new but terrifying, and he asked the oarsmen to anchor the boat where they were, without approaching any nearer, that he might converse at leisure with da Gama on those matters affecting the Portuguese of which he had had report.

His delight was evident as he engaged the Captain on one topic after another, now enquiring concerning the wars his country had waged so gloriously against the followers of Islam, now asking about the peoples who dwelt in that last of the Hesperias, or about their neighbours, or about the route he had followed across the seas.

'But before anything else, brave Captain,' he said, 'tell us faithfully all about your own country, what part of the world it lies in, what its climate is like, who your ancestors were and what the beginnings of such a powerful kingdom. Tell us how the Portuguese have fared in war right from the start, for, without knowing, I still know that they have done great things. Tell us too of your long peregrinations over the angry ocean, and what strange and barbarous practices you have observed in this uncouth Africa of ours.

'Speak freely, for we have a whole new day before us: the winds have gone to rest, and there is not a ripple on the sea. And the occasion is no more propitious than my desire is keen to hear your tale, for who is there who does not know by repute the remarkable achievements of your race? Nor does the sun shine so obliquely on us here in Malindi that you should think us dull of heart and intellect beyond a proper appreciation of noble deeds.

'The giants in their arrogance made war on Olympus, if

in vain. Theseus and Pirithous were bold, in their ignorance, to assault Pluto's dark and fearsome kingdom. If history records such daring enterprises as the laying siege to both heaven and hell, to assail the fury of the ocean is another no whit less hazardous or renowned. Herostratus set fire to Chersiphron's masterpiece, the temple of Diana in Ephesus, merely that men everywhere should talk of him. When even such spurious deeds can confer notoriety, how much more legitimate is his hope of undying glory who performs exploits as memorable as yours!'

CANTO

3

I RELY on you, Calliope, to reveal to me what it was da Gama told the king of Malindi. My devotion to you you know: give me in return, though I am but a mortal, the gift of divine accents and immortal song. And may Apollo forget the charms of Daphnes, Clyties, and Leucothoes and be more faithful to you in future than he has been in the past.

For it is to you, Nymph, that I must look to see my enterprise through as the people of Portugal deserve. Let the world know and see that the same inspiration is to be found in the waters of the Tagus as in the fountain of the Muses on Mount Helicon. Come-down from the slopes of Pindus, for I feel already the baptism of Apollo. You would not have me call you afraid for your beloved Orpheus, lest in the result he be overshadowed.

All sat hanging on da Gama's lips. For a moment, lost in thought, he was silent. Then he lifted his gaze and began. 'You bid me tell you, King, of my people and their for-bears. You want me, not to relate some impersonal history, but to sing the praises of my own race. It is a customary and desirable thing that men should extol the valour of others; I fear none the less that it may ill become me to exalt that of my fellow-countrymen, and that such praise may be held open to suspicion. I fear too – rather, I know – that, however much time we have, it will not be enough to tell all.

'Still, you have commanded, and it is your due. I obey, even if it does go against the grain, and I shall try to be brief. What most persuades me is the thought that there will be no temptation for me to lie in anything I say, for such is the record that, however much I may relate, more will remain untold. I begin, then. And, to satisfy your curiosity in an orderly fashion, I shall deal first with the country itself, and then with its war-stained history.

'Proud Europe lies between the tropic of Cancer and the Arctic zone, where the cold is as intense as the heat is here on the equator. To the north and west it is bounded by the ocean, to the south by the Mediterranean Sea. To the east lies Asia, from which it is divided by the long and sinuous course of the River Don, that flows into the Sea of Azov, and by the Aegean Sea, witness once of the might of the Greeks, where the traveller today will scarce find a memory of Troy and its triumphs. In the region nearest the Pole rise the Hyperborean Mountains and the Rhipaeans, source of the Don, whose name derives from the winds of Aeolus that blow unceasingly about them.

'In those latitudes the sun's rays are powerless against the perpetual snow on the hills and the frozen seas and rivers. The Scythians live there in great numbers, the same who, a long time ago, fought a fierce war with the Egyptians over the question which country had been the cradle of mankind. How easily man's judgement falls into error! Had these, who were so far off the mark, been concerned to know the truth, they would have enquired of the plain of Damascus.

'In those parts are to be found too Lapland and the island of Scandinavia, where bleak Norway still boasts the victories of its Lombards on the soil of Italy. And there, until winter ice puts an end to navigation, Prussians, Swedes, and

Danes sail the waters of the Baltic Sea. Between the Baltic and the Don dwell a number of uncouth races, Ruthenians, Moscovites, Livonians, all once known as Sarmatians. In the Hercynian Forest live Polish Marcomans. Saxons, Bohemians, and Pannonians are subject races of the German Empire, with various others who dwell along the Rhine, the Danube, the Ems, and the Elbe.

'The sturdy Thracians, whose land is the favourite abode of Mars, inhabit the region between the lower Danube and the Hellespont. Here the Balkans and Rhodope lie under the yoke of the Turk. Even Byzantium now owns his shameful sway, a grievous insult to the memory of the great Constantine. The peoples of Macedonia, watered by the Vardar, come next; and after them the land famous for its society, its intellect, its valour, that fount of eloquence and imagination, illustrious Greece, whose fame alike in arms and in letters has soared to the heavens. Dalmatia follows; then Venice, proud in spite of its lowly origins, jutting out into the gulf where once Antenor came to build.

'And there a peninsula begins whose bold inhabitants have in the past overrun a number of nations. Strong of arm, they are a people of genius in the arts of peace no less than of war. The sea encircles their land almost completely, high mountains the rest. Down its centre run the Apennines, that figure gloriously in its wars in defence of their native soil. But now that it is become the seat of the Popes, keepers of the keys of Heaven, it has lost its martial spirit and the practice of war and has laid aside the power it once wielded; for God loves the humble in spirit.

'Beyond Italy lies Gaul with its four rivers, the Seine, the Rhone, the Rhine, and the Garonne, a land made known throughout the world by the conquests of Caesar. It is bounded to the south by the mountains where the nymph Pyrene lies buried. Tradition relates that once they were set on fire, and ran rivers of gold and silver.

'And now behold the very head of all Europe, noble Spain, a country with a stirring history of dominion and glory interspersed with many a turn of the wheel of fortune. But no fickleness of fate can ever deal it a blow, whether by force or guile, that the valour and daring of its inhabitants will not rebuff. It lies opposite Mauretania, where the Mediterranean is all but closed at the famous strait that commemorates the last labour of Hercules.

'Spain too is all but an island, but its greatness is not that of one nation only but of several, all of them such in worth and nobility that each thinks itself more excellent than the rest. First there is Aragon, famous for its conquest of turbulent Naples; then Navarre; Asturias, that bulwark against the Moslem; cautious Galicia; Leon; Castile the peerless, cast by destiny to recover Spain for Christendom and to exercise hegemony over the others; and finally Seville and Granada.

'And if Spain is the head of Europe, Portugal, set at its western extremity, where land ends and sea begins, is as it were the crown on the head. Righteous Heaven willed that here the struggle with the miscreant Moslem should prosper exceedingly and end with his total expulsion; and now even on the burning sands of Africa he is allowed no peace.

'There is my happy, my beloved country. If God but grant me to return to it in safety, this enterprise accomplished, then let me die, for I shall die content. Lusitania it was formerly called, from either Lusus or Lysa, the sons – some say, companions – of Bacchus, who were the earliest inhabitants.

'From this land sprang the shepherd Viriato, of whose virile exploits his very name is suggestive. His fame none will ever cast into the shadow, since mighty Rome herself was no match for him. And as the years passed the land came, by Heaven's decree, to rank as a great kingdom and to play no mean part in the world. This was how it befell.

'There was a king of Spain, Alfonso VI, who waged unceasing war on the Saracens and by force of arms and subtle tactics inflicted on them great loss of life and territory. These exploits carried his fame as if on wings from Gibraltar to the Caucasus, and from divers lands there came knights offering to fight and to risk their lives under his banner. It was a genuine devotion to the faith, rather than the spur of honours and applause, that led them thus to turn their backs on home and country; and when they had rendered signal service in battle Alfonso saw to it that they were fitly recompensed.

'One of these, Henrique by name – the second son, men say, of a famous king of Hungary – was given Portugal as his reward, a territory at that time not yet on men's lips nor even held of much worth. As a further token of his regard, Alfonso gave him too his daughter Teresa in marriage; and with her the Count took possession of his new domains. From there he continued, like the valorous knight he was, to wage war on the Moslems, winning notable victories and constantly expanding his frontiers; and soon God rewarded him with the birth of a son who was to confer new lustre on the proud name of this warlike country.

'Henrique took part in the capture of the Holy City [in the First Crusade], and saw the waters of the Jordan where Jesus was baptized. But once his leader, Godefroi de Bouillon, had overrun Judaea he met with no further opposition, and many of those who had accompanied him returned home, Henrique among them. Eventually Henrique died, and his soul returned to God who gave it. In his son, who was still of a tender age, he left a copy of himself, one of the world's bravest men. From such a father such a son was but to be expected.

'Here ancient tradition has it – whether it is to be believed I do not know, for in matters of such antiquity there can never be certainty – that the mother seized the land for herself and married again, leaving her fatherless child disinherited; for, she said, the territories in question were all hers only, having been given to her by her father as a marriage portion.

'Prince Afonso – he had been called after his grandfather – thus saw himself excluded from any say in his own country, which his mother and her new husband were not merely ruling but devouring. His combative nature was aroused, and he fell to planning how he might recover it. After some thought he decided on his course of action, and immediately set about carrying it out.

'Mother and son met in civil war on the blood-stained field of Guimarães. It was an unnatural mother who could deny her son both her love and his own estates, and in her pride she could not see how deeply she sinned against God and against a mother's heart. But love with her was more sensual than anything else. Cruel Progne and Medea of the black art both avenged on their innocent children the sins of their husbands; Teresa's crime was blacker still. Evil incontinence and ugly greed are the common motives of such behaviour. One of them was enough to make Scylla kill her aged father; Teresa was driven by both equally when she turned against her son.

'The prince won the day against his stepfather and his iniquitous mother; and now at last he ruled over the land that at first had fought against him. It was then that, letting anger cloud his judgement, he condemned his mother to rigorous imprisonment. But a son's obligation to treat his parents with profound respect is not one that can ever be set aside, and in due course God punished his offence.

'Proud Castile meantime was quick to resent the insult to Teresa, and sent an army against her son. It was a fierce encounter, for he was as stout of heart as he was short of men; but Heaven was on his side, and he held his own against the enemy's onslaught and in the end repulsed them. The Castilians took their trouncing; but soon they came back with a still larger army and besieged him in the same Guimarães.

'This time Afonso was taken ill-prepared, and might well have fallen into their hands had not his faithful tutor Egas Moniz risked his own life to save him. The loyal vassal knew that his master could not put up an effective resistance, and went to the Castilian with an undertaking that if the siege were lifted he would himself induce Afonso to submit. The enemy accepted Moniz's assurances and good faith, and raised the siege.

'But the haughty youth would not submit to another's yoke, and when the time was come and the king of Castile was already awaiting his arrival to take the oath of fealty to him, Moniz saw that his word to the Castilian was not going to be honoured.

'Since he could not himself compel compliance, he determined to atone to the enemy with his life, and, accompanied by his wife and children, set out to redeem his pledge. Barefooted and clad only in shirts, their appearance was such as to move rather to compassion than to vengeance. "Great King," he said, "if you seek to visit retribution on my rash confidence, here I am, ready to pay for it with my life. Here are my hands and tongue, that swore and confirmed the oath. Exact from them the cruellest torment or mode of death you know, or that Sinis or Phalaris and his bull can suggest. These innocents are my wife and children: I place them too in your power, should a noble and generous heart find satisfaction in putting the helpless to death."

'Moniz stood before the indignant monarch like a condemned man who lays his head on the block and, having already tasted death in life, calmly awaits the executioner's stroke. But the king was touched to see such rare loyalty, and at length allowed his anger to give way to pity. It was in truth a surpassing tribute to the fidelity of the Portuguese. Zopyrus the Persian did no more when he cut off his own ears and nose as a ruse to capture Babylon; at which the great Darius said repeatedly, sighing, that he would have preferred his Zopyrus whole to twenty Babylons.

'Prince Afonso now directed his martial efforts against the Moslems who held the lands to the south of the Tagus, that famous and delightful river. Pitching his camp on the field of Ourique, he confronted the enemy with a confidence based only on God, for he was outnumbered by perhaps a hundred to one. Any considered judgement would have held such boldness sheer temerity. There were five Moslem kings drawn up against him, all experienced in the hazards of war; one Ismar was their leader. In their ranks were warrior-maidens following their lovers to battle, like the Amazons who under Penthesilea gave such stout help to the Trojans, or those who lived on the banks of the Thermodon.

'The rays of dawn were shining cold and serene, chasing the stars from the sky, when Afonso was heartened by a vision of Christ on the cross. He knelt in adoration, all aflame with the ardour of faith, then shouted: "Reveal thyself to the infidels, O Lord, to the infidels, not to me, who already believe in thy might!" The miracle so fired the spirit of his troops that straightway they acclaimed the worthy and well-beloved prince as their rightful king, and in full view of the redoubtable enemy forces rent the heavens with their cries: "Hail, Afonso, King of Portugal, hail!"

'On the hill-side you may sometimes see a fierce mastiff urged on with shouts to attack a bull. The bull will rely on powerful thrusts with its horns, the dog on its agility. Barking, it takes a bite now at the enemy's ear, now at its flank; finally it sinks it teeth in its throat and snaps it, and the huge animal's might is in the dust. Such was the new king's attack on the barbarous hordes. His valour was keyed to a new pitch by the signal favours he had just received from God and his own people; and his men were no less spirited.

'The infidel dogs raised the alarm in a flurry of shouting and excitement; trumpets and other martial instruments were still blaring forth even as they seized their bows and lances, for the surprise of the assault had cast them into confusion.

'It was as though, with a north wind blowing, a fire were to break out on a sun-scorched plain and sweep through the dry brushwood: the shepherds, awakened from their nap, hurriedly round up their flocks and make for the village. So now the Moslems snatched at their weapons at random. They did not turn tail. Standing their ground with calmness, they threw their cavalry at the Portuguese, who received them unflinchingly on their lances. Some they unseated, tumbling them off more dead than alive; others turned and fled, calling on the Koran for help.

'There followed a succession of terrifying encounters, such as might shake a mountain from its base. Fearsome blows were dealt, and horses careered madly about the field. All the fury of war was let loose. The thrusts of the Portuguese played havoc with the enemy's harness, breast-plates and coats of mail. Heads went rolling on the ground, arms and legs parted company alike with owner and with sense of feeling, men lay disembowelled, the pallor of death on their features. Rivers of blood drowned nature's green and white in red. The infidel's forces were broken utterly, and he had lost the day.

'The triumphant Portuguese gathered in the spoils and trophies, and Afonso tarried for the customary three days on the field. It was here that, in token of the victory, he proudly adorned his white buckler with the design of five shields in bright blue, signifying the five kings he had van-quished. And within the five shields, disposed in the form of a cross, he commemorated further the divine help he had been vouchsafed by depicting in a different colour the thirty pieces of silver for which Christ was betrayed, five in each shield, the shield in the centre counting twice.

'Afonso did not wait long after this notable triumph before launching an attack on Leiria, which had already been won from the enemy and lost again. He recaptured it, and with it the stronghold of Arronches and the noble city of Santarem on the Tagus. Soon Mafra fell too, and Cintra, perched on the cool heights of Cynthia, in whose fountains the nymphs hide from the gentle snares of Cupid, eager to set even the springs afire with the ardent passion.

'And now it was fair Lisbon's turn, that queen among cities the world over, founded by the same Ulysses whose guile reduced Troy to ashes. Lisbon, whose might the seas now own, bowed then to the might of the Portuguese.

They were aided in the taking of it by a fleet that had come out of northern parts, from the regions of the Elbe and the Rhine and from Britain, on a holy crusade against the Saracen. These vessels sailed into the Tagus and joined forces with Afonso, whose fame by now had reached to the very skies, and together they laid siege to the city.

'It took five months of fierce and costly fighting before it surrendered, for the besieged were as desperate as the besiegers were resolute and dauntless. Nevertheless it surrendered, the city that was never taken even by the barbarian hordes of Vandals from the North who once extended the terror of their sway to the Ebro and the Tagus and as far as the Guadalquivir, where they gave their name to Andalusia.

'With the fall of Lisbon and the ever-growing renown of the Portuguese, what other city could hope to hold out? Soon all Extremadura was theirs, Obidos, Alemquer with its river gurgling through the streets, Torres Vedras. The famous cornlands across the Tagus were likewise overrun, and as Elvas, Moura, Serpa, Alcácer do Sal fell one after the other, the Moslem peasant realized that he would till the land no more. Noble Evora, the seat once of the rebel Sertorius, famous now for the royal aqueduct with its hundreds of imposing arches, was captured by the bold Giraldo the Fearless.

'Afonso was incapable of repose. If life were short, he would merge it in the longer life of fame. In revenge for the Moslem destruction of Trancoso he now marched on Beja; and when, before long, it surrendered, his irate troops put the population to the sword. Palmela and the fishing-port of Sezimbra were the next to fall; and here he had the good fortune to destroy too a powerful army that was hastening to the latter's relief.

'The encounter took place on the mountain-side, within earshot of Palmela, and caught the enemy unawares. The king of Badajoz was a towering figure as he advanced at the head of four thousand horse and innumerable foot, a fearsome array of warlike accoutrements and garnishings of gold. But just as, in May, the bull in rut will leap out on the careless passer-by with the blind fury of a jealous lover, so now Afonso, suddenly showing himself, attacked the unsuspecting army on the march and inflicted on it a devastating defeat. The Moslem king took thought only to his life and fled; his army, struck with a panic terror, did its best to follow. The cause of all the havoc was a body of sixty horse.

'The indefatigable Afonso lost no time in following up his victory. From all over the kingdom he assembled troops seasoned in constant campaigning and marched on Badajoz itself, where he launched an attack so bold and skilful that it too soon succumbed and went to join the others.

'Until now God had always guarded Afonso in the midst of dangers. Whether to give the sinner opportunity to make amends, or for other reasons that we cannot penetrate, he often bides his time before visiting man with his displeasure. But at last he allowed the mother's curse to come home to the son who had held her captive. For in Badajoz Afonso was himself besieged by the Leonese, on the ground that it lay within their sphere of conquest. He accepted the challenge with spirit and hastened to join issue with the besiegers; but, as happens not infrequently, his pertinacity cost him dear, for he caught and broke his leg in an iron gate, and not merely lost the battle but was taken prisoner.

'Great Pompey need not have grieved to see his illustrious exploits crumble in ruin when Nemesis decreed that he should suffer condign defeat at Caesar's hands. From the Phasis in the north to Syene in the south, from Arcturus to the equator his name was feared. He won victories in Arabia and over the fierce Sarmatians, against Colchis of the Golden Fleece and the Cappadocians, in Judaea, the home of the true God. Peace-loving Sophenians, cruel Cilicians, Armenia with its sacred Mount Ararat, where the Tigris and the Euphrates have their source, all the lands, in short, that stretch from the Atlantic Ocean to the soaring Taurus Mountains saw in him a conqueror. What cause had he for astonishment that there should befall him one reverse on the field of Thessaly? Let him consider the proud, triumphant Afonso, everywhere victorious and in the end humbled to the dust. For such was the will of Providence, that a wife's father should bring low the one, a daughter's husband the other.

'Such was the tardy chastisement meted out to Afonso by divine justice. Later, at Santarem, he was again beleaguered, this time by the presumptuous Saracens, but in vain. One of his last acts was to transfer the remains of the blessed martyr St Vincent from the promontory that bears his name to Lisbon. Age was now taking its toll of him, and he passed his mission on to his son, bidding him resume the campaign in the lands south of the Tagus.

'Sancho proved a brave and spirited youth. He led his forces south, and at Triana made the Guadalquivir run red with the blood of the infidel. This victory whetted his appetite, and he did not rest till he had achieved another, no less resounding, over the Moslem army that was besieging Beja. A second time his ambition was speedily accomplished.

'Such repeated disasters were giving the enemy cause for reflection, and now he planned how he might avenge them.

From Mount Atlas – the giant who supported the heavens on his shoulders until he was petrified by the sight of Medusa's head – from Cape Espartel, from Tangier, that was once the abode of Antaeus, from Ceuta, from all over the kingdom of Mauretania came reinforcements to the sound of the hoarse Moorish trumpet.

'The Caliph of Morocco crossed over into Portugal with thirteen kings of note, all subject to his suzerainty, in his train. Sancho was at Santarem, and the invaders set out to invest him there, working what destruction they could on the way, though the Christians allowed them but little opportunity. Nor did fortune favour them overmuch at Santarem either.

'With battering-ram, catapult, hidden mine, they rained attacks in their fury, invoking every stratagem they knew. It availed them nothing, for Sancho had lost none of his father's valour and resource. His spirit and judgement were equal to every contingency, and, probe where they might, the enemy met the same fierce resistance everywhere.

'Afonso was then living in Coimbra on the banks of the Mondego, in the retirement imposed on him by age, when he heard that the infidels had thrown an army against his son at Santarem. But age had not robbed him of his capacity for quick decisions, and he set out at once to the relief with a body of veteran troops. Joining forces, father and son fought with customary Portuguese ferocity, and soon routed the foe. The field was strewn with the cloaks and hoods, the horses and harness of dead Moslems: it was a rich haul. Those who survived fled from the field, and lost no time in getting back to Africa. The Caliph did not fly: he was dead. In such a turning of the tables it was clear that the divine favour had counted for more than numbers, and the Portuguese gave all praise and thanks to God who had granted them the victory.

'And so the aged and illustrious Afonso continued triumphant to the end, until he was himself defeated by the sheer weight of years. Pale death laid her chill hand upon his enfeebled body, and he paid his dues at last to the gloomy goddess. The headlands wept for him, the rivers grieved and their waters swamped the fields with tearful tribute. But his deeds of valour had winged their way to universal esteem, and in his own country the echoes will ever resound with his name. They cannot, alas, bring him back.

'It was evident from Sancho's prowess in the field that he was destined to tread in Afonso's footsteps. He had already proved himself, in his father's lifetime, when he inflicted defeat on the Moslem king of Andalusia and made the Guadalquivir run with the enemy's blood, and still more when those who laid fruitless siege to him in Beja felt the weight of his right arm. And now, proclaimed king, he did not let many years pass before investing Silves, in the midst of lands still under Moslem cultivation.

'Once more help came from a substantial and well-armed German fleet which happened to be passing on its way to the Holy Land, that had again fallen into the hands of the infidel. For the Moslems had cut off the Holy City's water supply, and its defenders under Guy de Lusignan had been compelled by the torments of thirst to yield it to the Sultan. Frederick of Germany – Barbarossa, they called him – was now leading a powerful army to the rescue, and this fleet was sailing to take part in the crusade when a contrary wind forced it to seek harbour. The two causes being one at bottom, the newcomers resolved to give Sancho their support, thus repeating what had befallen his father at the taking of Lisbon. Silves fell, and its stout defenders either submitted to the yoke or perished.

'Nor were these victories over the Moslem the whole story. For Sancho carried war too into the territories of Leon, that were already indeed not unfamiliar with it, and reduced proud Tuy to his sway. Many neighbouring towns as well he humbled by might of arms. It was in the midst of these triumphs that grim death pounced upon him.

'Sancho's son and heir, Afonso II, third king of Portugal, was held by all in high regard. It was in his reign that Alcácer do Sal was finally recovered from the Moslems, who now paid with their lives for having won it back some time previous.

'To Afonso there succeeded Sancho II, a mild and shiftless character whose shiftlessness reached such extremes that, where he should have ruled, he was himself ruled by others. In the end his dependence on favourites allowed a rival claimant to oust him from the throne, for as he followed their counsel in all things, so he tolerated all their vices.

'His depravity, it is true, was never that of a Nero, who could take a youth to wife and commit incest with his own mother. Nor were his cruelties and exactions: he never set his own capital on fire. Heliogabalus far outdid him in wickedness, and Sardanapalus in effeminacy. He never tyrannized his people as did the tyrants of Sicily, nor was he a Phalaris in inventing new torments. But his country was a proud one, accustomed to monarchs who were sovereign in all things. It does not obey, nor will it tolerate, a king who is not outstanding above all his subjects in excellence.

'And so the kingdom passed to his brother the Count of Boulogne, who was formally proclaimed king when the indolent Sancho died. Afonso the Brave he was called; and after seeing to the security of the country he too set himself to extend its frontiers, for his ambitious nature was not to be contained in so little territory. The Algarve had already been assigned to him in a marriage settlement, and of this he now recovered a large part from the Moslems, whom he expelled. Their fortunes in war were on the decline, and Afonso, thanks to his skill and prowess in battle, lived to see all Portugal free and sovereign at last. Moslem might was never again to raise its head among the descendants of Lusus.

'Dinis, who followed, showed himself a worthy scion of so stalwart a father. In him the noble qualities and the fame of Alexander the Great were surpassed. For with his reign came peace, golden, divine peace, and the country flourished with new laws, customs, and constitutions that shed a splendour over the tranquil land. Dinis was the first to make of Coimbra a seat of learning and to induce the Muses to leave Mount Helicon for the gentle swards of the Mondego. Thither Apollo transferred all that Athens had stood for, and it was there in future that the crown of nard and laurel interwoven with gold was to be won.

'He was a builder too. Many a fine town, many a stout fortress and castle he raised up again. His great edifices and towering battlements altered the whole face of the country. And then, in the fulness of age, he died, leaving a son Afonso IV, brave and well-endowed, it is true, but headstrong.

'Afonso always harboured in his heart a firm and serene contempt for the pride of Castile. It was never a mark of the Portuguese to fear an enemy just because they were outnumbered. Yet when a new invasion from Africa descended upon Castile, in the hope of again overrunning Spain, he hastened to give help.

'The Saracen hordes who crossed over to join those of Granada on the field of Tartessos were as the sands of the sea, far outnumbering the Assyrians of Semiramis as they swarmed over the plains of the Hydaspes, or the Huns of Attila, self-styled the scourge of God, when he spread terror throughout Italy. The Castilian monarch, contemplating this unassailable array, feared, more than his own death, a repetition of the earlier eclipse of Christian Spain. He resolved to ask the Portuguese for succour, and sent as envoy his own wife, Afonso's beloved daughter.

'The lovely Maria was beautiful as ever, but there was no gladness in her face when she entered her father's palace. Her eyes were bathed in tears, her angelic tresses hung in disarray over her ivory shoulders, as to her father, who received her joyfully, she sobbed out her message.

' "The king of Morocco has mobilized all the tribes of Africa for the conquest of Spain. It is a fearsome assemblage. So multitudinous an army has never been seen since the first waves lapped against the beach. The fury they threaten might make the dead turn in their graves: it strikes terror to the heart of the living. He whom you gave me as husband has scant forces at his command, and in defence of his panic-stricken country he stands exposed to the full weight of the enemy's blows. Unless you hasten to his help, you will see me at once without a husband and without a kingdom, condemned to the hapless melancholy of a widow dispossessed of all she held dear.

' "With fear of you, my father, the rivers of Morocco turn to ice. Do not waste time: hurry to the rescue of the wretched Castilians. If it be a true father's love I read in your welcoming face, help us, and quickly, or you may not find my husband still alive."

'It was in just such terms that Venus once implored her

father Jupiter's favour for her son Aeneas as he voyaged; and so moved was Jupiter then that, the thunderbolt falling from his hands, he granted his daughter all she asked, and regretted only that she should ask so little.

'Soon the plains of Evora were thick with squadrons of troops, their lances, swords and armour flashing in the sun. The horses neighed, and hearts grown accustomed to peace were incited to battle by the resounding echoes of the embannered trumpets. In the midst stood Afonso, a commanding figure, and not merely in virtue of his royal insignia, for he towered head and shoulders above the rest. His very look breathed courage into the timorous. And so he crossed into Castile, accompanied by Castile's gentle queen, his daughter.

'The two Alfonsos met at length near Tarifa, confronting an array of infidel forces so vast that it was scarcely to be contained on plain and hillside. Were it not for the firm conviction that Christ was fighting on the side of his faithful, there was none among the Christians that day so valiant or so strong that he would not have been a prey to apprehension. The Ishmaelites laughed to see the opposing forces so puny; already in imagination they were dividing out the land among themselves. But their title to it was about as valid as it was to the name of Saracen, for it was not from Sarah but from Hagar that they were descended.

'The giant Goliath waxed arrogant once, when he saw the shepherd David stand defenceless before him, armed only with his sling and a stout heart, and hurled contemptuous taunts at the slender, ill-garbed youth. Was not King Saul himself afraid of him, and with reason? David, swinging his sling, disillusioned him, and taught him how much more potent is faith than brute force. The miscreant Moslems made the same mistake now, contemning the

95

power of the Christians and not realizing that behind it lay the might of Heaven itself, to which hell with all its horrors must bow. So fortified, the Castilian, deploying all his skill, took the offensive against the king of Morocco, while the Portuguese, who feared no one, brought home to the king of Granada what fear meant.

'The havoc was great as lance and sword resounded on coat of mail, one side calling on Mahomet, the other on Santiago. The cries of the wounded rent the heavens as they lay wallowing in a sea of blood where others, having barely escaped the sword, were drowned. So devastating was the Portuguese onslaught on those of Granada that neither breastplate of steel nor other defence could withstand it, and soon they were completely routed. But the victors were not content with a victory so easily won, and hastened to the side of the Castilians as they battled with the forces from Africa.

'The sun was sinking towards the western sea, and with the appearance of the evening star that great and unforgettable day was drawing to a close, when the two valiant monarchs between them finally overthrew that vast and fearsome array. Memory cannot recall another such victory, nor one accompanied by such slaughter. Marius did not slay the quarter part when at Aix he made his troops slake their thirst in water running red with the enemy's blood; nor Hannibal, that most bitter of Rome's enemies from birth, when after Cannae he filled a bushel measure with rings from the Roman dead. Titus may have dispatched as many to the nether regions when he cleansed the Holy City of Jews, but that was by divine permission, out of the wrath of God, and not by force of arms, for so it had been foretold by the prophets and confirmed afterwards by Jesus.

'From this auspicious triumph Afonso returned to Portugal, thinking to enjoy peace with no less glory than he had won in the rigours of war. Instead there befell the grievous tragedy, the actors in which will always live in men's minds, of the forlorn and hapless queen who only after death was raised to the throne. It was love, and nothing but love, whose pitiless yoke weighs so heavily on human hearts, that brought about her death, the death one metes out to a treacherous enemy. When men say that love's thirst is not to be assuaged by the saddest of tears, it is because the cruel tyrant prefers its altars to run with the blood of its victims.

'The lovely Inês de Castro was living in tranquil retirement, enjoying the sweet fruits of life in that happy state of blind illusion that fortune never wills should endure for long. As she strolled by the beloved banks of the Mondego, with whose waters she mingled many a tear, the swards and slopes heard often the name she bore written on her heart. And there the fond remembrances of her that her Pedro carried in his bosom struck an echo, memories that in absence ever conjured her up before his eyes, by night in sweet delusive dreams, by day in winged thoughts. All he dwelt on and all he saw evoked in him only recollection of that delight.

'Divers matches with great ladies and princesses were proposed for him, but he rejected them all, for true love, having found its object, can make no place for others. Afonso, now grown old and pensive, took note of his son's extremity of devotion and of his obstinacy in the matter of marriage; and, giving ear to the murmurings of the people, he resolved to put Inês to death as the only way of releasing him from her toils. He conceived that the spilling of innocent blood could extinguish the fires of an unshakable passion. What madness was it that allowed the raising against a gentle, defenceless lady of the glorious sword that had withstood the fury of the Moslem onslaught?

'The dread executioners dragged Inês before the king. He was already persuaded to pity, but the people persisted in their calumnies and their hate and constrained him to seal her doom. Inês spoke. Her words were sad and pitiful, sprung solely from grief and longing for her prince and their children whom she must leave behind; for this, and not death, was what she feared. While one of the caitiffs tied her hands, she raised to Heaven her tearful, compassionate eyes, then fixed them on the infants she so loved and had so tenderly cared for, and whom as a mother she could not bear to see orphaned, and at last addressed their cruel grandfather:

' "Nature made the brute beasts cruel from birth, and endowed the birds of the air with a mind intent only on rapine; yet even so Semiramis was brought up by doves, while Romulus and Remus, the founders of Rome, were suckled by a she-wolf, in proof that tenderness for little children is a sentiment not unknown to them. You have the face and the heart of a human, if it can be accounted human to put a weak and helpless woman to death merely because her heart belongs to him who loves her. Let the fate of these infants cause you to reflect, if the obscure death to which you would condemn their mother does not. Let their piteousness, and my pity for them, move you, since my innocence leaves you cold.

' "Your victories over the Moslem showed that you knew how to deal out death by fire and the sword. Show now that you know too how to be clement and to grant life to one who has done no wrong that she should lose it. If, being guiltless, I still deserve punishment, sentence me to grim, perpetual exile among the snows of Scythia or under Libya's burning sun, where I may shed an eternity of tears. Expose me to the ferocity of lions and tigers: perchance among them I may find the pity I have been denied among men. There, with my whole heart and will still centred on him who is my life, I shall bring up his children to be the solace of their mother's grief."

'The king was kindly at heart and would have spared her life, for her words touched him deeply. But fate had already spoken: the headstrong people would have none of it, and some there present themselves drew their swords, openly holding the deed politic. Knights, they called themselves; butchers, rather, to show such savagery towards one of the fair sex.

'So once the hard-hearted Pyrrhus raised his sword against the beauteous Polyxena, her aged mother's last remaining joy, at the bidding of the shade of Achilles; and she, gazing on her distraught parent with eyes that radiated serenity, offered herself to the sacrifice with the gentle resignation of a lamb. With the like brutality these cruel assassins now plunged their swords into Inês's neck, that alabaster pedestal for the beauty that first smote her prince with love; and the white flowers at her feet, lately watered with her tears, turned red. Little did they reck, in the heat of their fury, of the retribution to come.

'Well might the sun that day have denied its light to such a scene, as once before at the grim banquet where Atreus served up to Thyestes his own offspring. From her dying lips the hollow valleys caught up the one word "Pedro", and echoed it over and over. The dainty camomile, plucked untimely and woven with wanton hands into a maiden's chaplet, soon loses its fragrance and the brightness of its hues. So chill death laid its hand on Inês: the roses ebbed from her cheeks, the bright complexion faded, sweet life itself had fled.

'The nymphs of the Mondego were long to remember, with sobbing, that dark dispatch; and their tears became a spring of pure water, that remembrance might be eternal. The fountain marks the scene of her earlier happiness, and is still known today by the name they gave it, "Inês the Lover". Lucky the flowers that are nurtured from such a source, its name telling of love, its water of tears.

'Pedro had not long to wait to see those wounds avenged. No sooner did he succeed to the throne than he took steps against the murderers, who had fled into Spain. He and his namesake Pedro the Cruel of Spain each had their enemies, and, by means of a pact like that once entered into by Octavian, Antony, and Lepidus, he secured the delivery of the fugitives into his hands.

'His was a rigorous rule. Thieves, murderers, adulterers he punished severely, his fierce and irate disposition knowing no greater pleasure than to repay crime with cruelty. He was concerned for justice, and was a bulwark of the towns against the exactions of the nobility. More robbers forfeited their lives at his instance than were ever accounted for by Hercules or Theseus.

'But Nature loves a paradox. Pedro's son Fernando was as gentle, as remiss, as negligent as he had been hard and just; and before long he had brought the kingdom to a perilous pass. For he neglected its defences, and Castile, pouncing on the opportunity, spread such devastation throughout the land that it seemed it must be totally destroyed. A weak king can sap the courage of a strong people. Fernando had succumbed to a blind infatuation for Leonor Teles de Meneses, whom he carried off from her husband and made his wife, and it may have been for this that he was punished. Perhaps it was simply that the character that yields itself up to criminal lust forfeits its vigour and strength.

'Examples abound to show that an unworthy love can weaken the strongest, and God has willed that for this sin many should pay the penalty. So the Trojans when they stole Helen, so Appius, and Tarquin. What was the cause of David's downfall, or of the destruction of the illustrious tribe of Benjamin? Pharaoh and Sarah, Shechem and Dinah tell the same story. Ask Hercules, as he sat at Omphale's feet clad in her garments, what a foolish and illicit passion does to valour. Or Marc Antony when he became so enamoured of Cleopatra. Or Hannibal when, at the height of his success, he let his fancy fall on a humble Apulian maid.

'Yet who perchance can shake himself free of the web that love spins so gently among the roses of a woman's cheeks, the snow of her skin, the gold of her hair, her alabaster neck? Who is proof against the exquisite beauty of a face that can turn the heart it has taken captive, not indeed to stone as did Medusa's, but into burning desire? What man can behold the gracious features, the confident glance, the gentle, angelic perfection that draws all hearts, and still hold out? They who are as yet fancy-free may judge Fernando guilty: such as have had experience of love will assuredly find excuses for him.

4

'THE night is dark, the wind howls, the tempest rages. But with morning comes light, and calm, and the hope of making harbour in safety; for the rising sun, as it vanquishes the darkness, frees men's minds too from the grip of fear.

'So it befell my country on the death of King Fernando. My countrymen had had but one wish, that someone might arise to avenge on their authors all the crimes and wrongs committed by those who had so cleverly exploited Fernando's remissness; and with the acclamation as their lawful king of the ever-illustrious João I, Pedro's only surviving heir, though a bastard, their wish was granted. That this was so ordained by Heaven a portent made abundantly clear. It happened in Evora, where a baby girl, suddenly endowed with speech, raised itself in its cradle and, hand in air, proclaimed: "Portugal, Portugal, behold your new king, Dom João!"

'With his accession the hatred that had taken possession of men's hearts found vent in violence. The people rose in their fury, spreading cruel havoc over the land and visiting with death the friends and relations of the adulterous Count of Ourem and of Queen Leonor who, after her husband's death, had indulged even more openly her guilty passion. The Count met the dishonourable death he deserved, being slain in cold blood before her eyes, and many another went the same way, for there was no quenching the burning lust for vengeance. The Bishop of Lisbon's holy orders availed him nothing: like Astyanax, he met his doom by being hurled from a high tower. Others likewise found protection neither in orders, nor in the sanctuary of the altar, nor in rank. Some were stripped naked in the streets and torn to pieces.

'Scenes such as these might well cast into the shadow the fearsome cruelties enacted at Rome by the ferocious Marius or, after he had taken flight, by his bloodthirsty rival Sulla. They provoked Leonor into appealing to Castile for help against the Portuguese, on the ground that her daughter was true heir to the throne. In so doing she made manifest to everyone her grief at the Count's death.

'Beatriz, the daughter, was married to Juan I of Castile, and he now claimed the kingdom. That Fernando, reputedly her father, really was so her mother's evil reputation left in some doubt. The claim sufficed, however, for the Castilian, who, upholding her right of succession, set about raising troops throughout his dominions to enforce it in battle.

'From Old Castile they came, the original kingdom of the legendary Brigo, and from the newer territories that Fernando I and the Cid Ruy Díaz had won back from the tyranny of the Moslems. The peasants of Leon, who had already given a good account of themselves against the infidel, once more forsook their ploughs, scorning the perils of war. From Seville on the Guadalquivir, the capital of Andalusia, came the descendants of the Vandals, confident that time had left their valour untarnished. Cadiz, that noble foundation of the Phoenicians of old, likewise sent its contingents, their banners bearing as device the pillars of Hercules.

'So too the illustrious and ancient city of Toledo, girdled

by the gently meandering Tagus that rises in the hills of Cuenca; Galicia, whose sons, as doughty as they are peasant-thrifty, armed fearlessly to meet a foe with whom they had already had exchanges; Biscay, a people rough in speech and quick to resent insult from strangers; Guipuzcoa and Asturias, that pride themselves on their iron-mines and the weapons they forge from them: all rallied to the support of their sovereign in the field.

'João for his part was nothing daunted, his strength welling up from his heart as Samson's from his hair, and with his scantier following he prepared for battle. If he took counsel with his leading nobles it was not that he wavered in his own resolve, but merely from the desire to assay their disposition, since where many are concerned a diversity of opinion is always to be looked for.

'And some did in fact advance views at variance with the common determination, their former valour having given way to an unwonted and discreditable disloyalty. Fear had chilled and numbed their hearts, driving out natural fidelity, until they were prepared to deny both their king and their country. Had it suited their interests, they would have denied, like Peter, their very God.

'Of their number the valiant Nuno Alvares Pereira was never one. Instead, when he saw that his own brothers were among them, he rounded angrily on them for their inconstancy and, laying hand on sword, threatened heaven, earth and sea as he harangued them in terms too forthright to admit of concern for elegance or rhetoric.

' "Is it possible," he cried, "that among Portuguese, with their proud history, there should be found any who are unwilling to make a stand for their native land? On many a field this nation has shown the whole world how to fight. Can there be among its sons those who would deny that it

still knows how to defend itself, who are prepared to refuse
it the faith and love, the bravery and skill of a Portuguese,
who could wish on any consideration to see their country
subject to a foreigner? It is unthinkable. Are you not still
the descendants of those who under the banner of the great
Afonso Henriques fought with such dash and courage as to
overthrow these same Spaniards, for all their martial spirit,
routing so many captains and their men and taking
prisoner seven noble counts, not to speak of booty?

'"Who was it, if not your own fathers and forefathers,
who enabled the great King Dinis and his son Afonso IV to
trample repeatedly under foot these very enemies who
would now do the same to you? If Fernando with his re-
missness, or his sins, has reduced you to such a craven state,
let your new king give you back your strength. Remember
that a change of ruler can work a change in his people too.
The king you have now proclaimed is such that, if your
own bravery but equal his, you may vanquish any enemy
you care to engage, how much more one you have already
defeated.

'"If this thought in itself be not enough to make you
shake off the empty fear that has eaten into your hearts,
well, let it tie your hands: I shall resist the alien yoke alone.
With my own followers and with this" – and he un-
sheathed his sword – "I shall ward off this harsh and in-
tolerable assault on a land that has never yet known
subjection. In the name of my king, of my grieving
country, and of that same loyalty that you deny it, I shall
win the day against not merely these adversaries but as
many others as dare oppose my sovereign."

'He might have been the young Cornelius Scipio facing
the broken survivors of Cannae at Canusium, when they
were more than half inclined to surrender to Hannibal's

conquering troops, and compelling them under threat of his sword to swear that never, while there was breath in their bodies, would they cease to fight for Rome. For such now was the effect of Nuno's harangue on his hearers. Even as they listened to his last words they shook off the chill, importunate dread that had frozen their courage, leapt to their horses, brandished and twirled their weapons and careered about the field shouting to the heavens: "Long live the illustrious king who sets us free!"

'As for the commoners, while some were voicing the general approval of the war in defence of the homeland, others set about polishing and refurbishing their arms that the years of peace had coated with rust, lining headpieces, testing breastplates, each man fitting himself out as best he could. Others again fashioned themselves garments of a thousand hues, adorning them with devices and mottoes in honour of their lady-loves.

'Such was the resplendent following with which João sallied forth at length from Abrantes, cool Abrantes the well-watered, thanks to the chill Tagus. Leading the van was a second Xerxes, one fit to have commanded the very armies of the East, redoubtable and countless as they were, with which the Persian once crossed the Hellespont. I speak, needless to say, of that same Nuno Alvares, true scourge of the insolent Castilians as Attila once was of Gauls and Italians.

'The right wing was under the well-merited command of another famous knight, Mem Rodrigues de Vasconcelos, and the left under that of Antão Vasques de Almada, who later became the noble Count of Avranches. Farther back, in the rear, the pennant of the valorous King João, with the shields and castles of his coat-of-arms, stood out in the view of all. So too did João, whose exploits were to cast those of Mars himself into the shade.

'The walls of Abrantes were lined meantime with mothers, sisters, sweethearts, wives, filled with apprehension, seized as it were with a joyous fear, who prayed and offered up vows of fasting and pilgrimage.

'Soon the martial squadrons found themselves confronted by the forces of the enemy, and both sides realized that neither could count on victory. The Castilians received them with a tremendous shouting. The Portuguese made reply with the blowing of trumpets and fifes and the beating of drums. It was mid-August, the harvest season when on the threshing-floor Ceres yields up her grain to the peasant and Bacchus draws the sweet must from the grape.

'And now the Castilians sounded the trumpet-call to arms, a mighty, fearsome blast that echoed to farthest Finisterre and caused the Guadiana's waters to flow upstream with dread. It was heard on the Douro and across the Tagus; the Tagus itself flowed more hesitantly to sea. Mothers, hearing the terrifying sound, clasped their children to their breasts.

'Even on the field many a face turned pallid as the blood hastened in friendly succour to the heart; for often, when peril is great, fear is greater still. If as much does not always appear, it is because in the fury of assailing and the hope of overthrowing the enemy one fails for the moment to appreciate how heavy, how irreparable, is the loss of limb or life.

'The front lines moved forward on both sides, and the doubtful issue was joined. The Portuguese were inspired by the thought that they were defending their country, the Spaniards by the hope of winning it. First to attract attention was the great Nuno himself, that very epitome of gallantry; one after another he engaged the foe and struck them down, until the ground seemed in fact to belong to those who so greatly coveted it. The air was thick with arrows, darts and bolts that hissed as they flew; the earth quivered and the valleys re-echoed to the pounding of galloping horses' hooves; lances were shivered, and the noise of men falling heavily in their armour was like claps of thunder. And still the enemy surged forward, in spite of all the losses he and his stalwarts inflicted.

'Then he saw his own brothers advance against him. It was an ugly and cruel dilemma. But Nuno was not to be taken aback, for he who rebels against his king and country will think little of seeking his brother's life. There were many such renegades in the enemy's spearhead who were now marching against brothers and relations. So it was in the civil wars of Caesar and Pompey. Sertorius, Coriolanus, Catiline and the others of past ages who with sacrilege in their hearts betrayed the land that gave them birth, and who are now doubtless paying the penalty in Pluto's dark domain, may know that there were times when even Portugal had her traitors.

'Such was the pressure of the enemy that our forward ranks gave ground. Nuno found himself like the fearless lion in the hills of Ceuta when hemmed in by the huntsmen of Tetuan. They threaten him with their lances and succeed in enraging, even in confusing him somewhat, but not in making him afraid. There is a terrifying look in his eyes; his savage nature and his anger alike forbid him to turn tail, impelling him rather to hurl himself against the wall of lances, even though it be continually reinforced. So now did Nuno, until his sword ran with the blood of his victims. Some of his own men perished too, for even bravery has its limits against such a multitude.

'But João was not unaware of the danger threatening his henchman. Wise leader that he was, he was everywhere, alive to everything, putting new heart into everyone with his presence and his words of cheer. Picture the fierce Numidian lioness that, having been out searching for food for her new-born cubs, returns to the lair to find some shepherd has stolen them and they are gone. She dashes madly hither and thither, quivering with rage; her roars rock the hills like thunder. Such was João as with a chosen few he dashed to the succour of his vanguard. "Hold your ground, my brave companions, my peerless knights," shouted the great-souled warrior. "The hope of freedom hangs on your lances! Here is your king, your fellow, ready at your head to brave the enemy for all his weapons and accoutrements!" And, poising his own lance with much deliberation, he hurled it so forcibly that not one but many of the enemy perished at the blow.

'His soldiers felt themselves nobly shamed. Fired with renewed ardour, they vied spiritedly with one another in defying the perils of combat. Blood spurted at the thrust of their lances, that did not stop at the enemy's mail but pierced his heart too. And so, dealing and receiving, they proclaimed their contempt for death itself.

'Among those they consigned to the Styx were the Master of the Order of Santiago, who had fought most valiantly, the Master of the other Order of Calatrava, a cruel man who wrought great havoc before he fell, and the renegade Pereiras who died blaspheming against Heaven and destiny. Many were the nameless commoners, and nobles too, who went to those nether regions where the insatiable Cerberus lies in wait for the souls of the dead. And, to the greater humbling of a proud and furious enemy, the very banner of Castile bit the dust at the foot of that of Portugal.

'The fierce encounter grew fiercer still, with thrusts and

cries and blood and slaughter. So numerous were the slain that the very flowers of the field changed colour. The enemy at length turned to fly, but there was no safety even in flight. Eventually the fury waned, and lances were returned to their rests. The king of Castile recognized his defeat, abandoned his purpose, and left the field to the victor, content not to be leaving behind his life as well.

'Those of his forces who had survived followed him on wings of fear, grieving deep down in their hearts at the loss of life and wealth, at the shame, the dishonour, the grim affront of seeing themselves defeated and despoiled. Some cursed and reviled whoever first invented war; others blamed the compelling thirst of the covetous breast that, from mere desire to possess what was another's, could expose a wretched people to the pains of hell and deprive so many hapless mothers and wives of their sons and husbands.

'King João, triumphant, remained on the field in glory for the customary period, and then with offerings and pilgrimages returned thanks to him who had enabled him to win the day.

'As for Nuno, his one desire was to leave behind him the reputation of invincibility in battle, and he set out forthwith for the lands across the Tagus. There too destiny favoured him and he carved his exploits to the measure of his desire; for in the frontier province of Andalusia the forces of Seville and of various neighbouring lords succumbed defenceless before his onslaught, yielding him up alike victory and booty.

'These were but the first of a long series of triumphs over the Spaniards, until at last, following on the Heaven-sent double marriage of the opposing kings to two illustrious English princesses, as gracious and comely as they were

illustrious, the victor conceded to the vanquished the peace
that all now longed for.

'But to the valiant heart, inured to war, it is irksome to
have no enemy at hand to attack. And so, there being none
now whom he might vanquish on land, João pitted him-
self against the ocean deep. He was the first monarch to go
forth from his native land and compel the African to recog-
nize by ordeal of battle how superior is the Christian faith
to that of Mahomet. Soon he had a thousand vessels
spreading their swelling sails to the wind as, skimming like
birds the silvery domain of restless, raging Tethys, they set
their course for the strait that was once to Hercules the
"Ne plus ultra". Seizing Mount Abyla and the noble city
of Ceuta, he expelled the miscreant Moslem and secured
the Peninsula against any repetition of the scurvy and
faithless manoeuvre whereby Count Julian had once in-
volved it in disaster.

'Portugal, alas, was not to enjoy for long so fortunate
a ruler, for before many years had passed death removed
him to the heavenly choir. For the defence of his people
God provided in his stead a noble family of princes who
were not merely to rule the land but to extend its frontiers
even further.

'Duarte's reign, it is true, was not notably auspicious.
Implacable destiny is wont thus to alternate good and evil,
joy and melancholy. What happy state has ever been
permanent? When has Fortune ever shown herself immu-
table? In this kingdom and under this king her fickleness
was no less in evidence. For Duarte lived to see his sainted
brother Fernando, a man vowed to the loftiest under-
takings, fall captive to the Saracens, to whom he sur-
rendered in order that the luckless Portuguese troops, sur-
rounded by the enemy, might go free. And when he could

have regained his freedom in return for the abandoning of Ceuta, he, a prince, set the common good above his own and, impelled by single-minded love of his country, chose to spend the rest of his days in captivity.

'Codrus of old deliberately sacrificed his life to achieve victory over the enemy. Regulus, rather than see his country overthrown, preferred to return to his captors. Fernando brought upon himself perpetual imprisonment that Spain and Portugal might rest free from fear. Neither Codrus nor Curtius, at mention of whose names men still marvel, nor those great patriots the Decii, did as much.

'Duarte's heir was another Afonso, bearer of a name now famous in our western land. He humbled to wretchedness the presumption of the barbarian across the strait, and, had he not ventured into Castile, would have been unbeaten on the field. Africa at least would have held it impossible that any foe should vanquish this terrible monarch. Hercules once plucked the golden apples of the Hesperides: Afonso seized the land where they grew, and the palm and the laurels of victory over the infidel were his. The doughty Moslem has not yet shaken off the yoke he placed on his neck. When he threatened Alcácer-Seguer, Tangier, Arzila, the barbarian hastened to their defence, but in vain. Redoubtable though their fortifications were, the Portuguese razed them and took the cities by storm, after their manner of demolishing every impediment in their way. In this campaign the fame of Portugal soared higher still with many a rare feat of arms deserving of worthy record.

'And then, fired with ambition and with that bittersweet, the glory of power, Afonso advanced a claim to the powerful kingdom of Castile and declared war on Fernando of Aragon. But the many and haughty peoples of that country, from Cadiz to the high Pyrenees, all recognized Fernando's authority and sent their contingents to swell his ranks. Afonso's son João, loath to remain at home, resolved to go to the aid of his ambitious father, and proved in fact a pillar of strength to him.

'In the upshot the bloodthirsty Afonso was able to withdraw, his brow still unclouded, from that tight corner. He had been defeated, but the verdict remained open none the less; for his son, a gentle, brave and spirited knight, inflicted heavy losses on the Spaniards and afterwards remained on the field for a whole day. So at Philippi, when they avenged the death of Caesar on his assassins, Octavian was defeated while Antony, his comrade-in-arms, emerged victorious.

'Afonso too died in due course, and João, second of the name and thirteenth king of Portugal, reigned in his stead. It was he who, in search of undying fame, attempted more than mortal man might hope to achieve by seeking to discover those same lands of the distant East that I go in search of now. His envoys travelled through Spain, France, Italy, taking ship finally at Naples, the city famous once as the birthplace of Parthenope, since when it has become the plaything of the Fates, tossed about from one power to another until now, in the fulness of time, they have bestowed distinction upon it under the illustrious suzerainty of Spain.

'From Naples they sailed over the waters of Sicily, first to Rhodes with its sandy beaches, then to Egypt with its cliffs made famous by the death of Pompey. Thence, by Memphis and the lands of the Nile, they reached Ethiopia, where the Christian religion still persists today, crossed that same Red Sea that the Israelites once passed over on foot, traversed the Nabathaean Hills, so called from Nebajoth son of Ishmael, and, leaving Arabia Petrea and

Deserta on one side, followed the myrrh-scented coasts of Arabia Felix.

'They came at length to the Persian Gulf, still redolent with memories of the confusion of Babel, and in whose waters mingle those of the Tigris and the Euphrates, two of the rivers believed to have their source in the Garden of Eden; and from there, across the ocean that set a term once to the ambition of the Emperor Trajan, they continued their quest for the sacred waters of the Indus, of which history still has much to tell. They encountered strange and unknown peoples, Carmanian, Gedrosian, Indian, and noted the changing manners and dress characteristic of each region. But there is no easy return from journeyings so rough and hazardous, and there in the end they died and there remained, never seeing their beloved native land again.

'It seemed that this so arduous enterprise was being reserved by Heaven to Manoel, in reward for his deserts. In the pursuit of it he was to perform great and famous deeds. Manoel, who succeeded João on the throne, was heir too to his lofty ambition, and no sooner were the reins of government in his hand than he set himself to achieve the mastery of the high seas.

'The stirring thought of this charge that his forefathers had bequeathed to him, men whose purpose had ever been to extend their country's sway, took unceasing possession of him; and one night, as daylight faded and the glistening stars appeared in the sky, inviting to repose, he lay down on his golden couch, where fancy so readily takes on an air of substance, and fell to turning over in his mind the responsibility of blood and office that was his. Soon gentle slumber closed his eyes, though without causing his heart to cease from dreaming, and while he dropped off into weary sleep Morpheus called up a succession of visions before his gaze.

'First he dreamt that he was being wafted up into the air, rising higher and higher until he came to the first sphere, of the moon, and could see a number of worlds spread out beneath him with nations densely peopled by fierce and outlandish races. Then, straining his eyes, he saw in the far distance, near where the sun rises, two deep limpid springs welling up in the midst of ancient, towering peaks. Wild birds and savage beasts monopolized those forbidding regions, a thousand forest trees and plants barring all passage or social intercourse. The rugged inhospitable mountains were sufficient evidence that never since the fall of Adam had human feet worn a track across them.

'And out of the two springs he seemed to see emerge, inclining their long strides in his direction, two men of great age and venerable if rustic aspect. Water dripped from the ends of their hair, spattering them all over, their skin was tanned and swarthy in hue, and they wore their long beards tangled and untrimmed. On their brows were chaplets woven of strange twigs and grasses.

'One bore himself wearily, as though he had made the longer journey; and in truth the water of his spring seemed to show, by its impetuous bubbling, that its source was elsewhere, just as the Alpheus makes its way underground from Arcadia to Syracuse in pursuit of Arethusa. He was the graver of the two in his bearing, and, while still a long way off, he addressed Manoel in a loud voice:

'"O King, to whose crown and kingdom so great a part of the earth is assigned, we too are not unknown to fame, and until now no alien yoke has ever oppressed our neck. Yet we would have you know that great tribute awaits you here, and that the time has come for you to send and receive it at our hands. I am the illustrious Ganges, whose waters have their source in the earthly paradise. My companion here is the Indus, that springs from this same mountain range you behold. We shall cost you, it is true, much stern fighting; but with perseverance you will eventually reap victories such as have never been seen before, and will reduce all the peoples in your path to fealty." The sacred river said no more, and both disappeared straightway.

'Manoel awoke with a start, to see the sun spreading its shining mantle over the sleepy western world and a new day painting the heavens red. He was strangely perturbed in his mind, and, summoning his counsellors, he told them of his vision and the figures he had seen. As he repeated the words of the venerable old man they were filled with amazement, and resolved there and then that an expedition should be got ready in which a chosen band of intrepid adventurers might set out across the ocean in search of these new climes and countries.

'For myself, I had always had a curious feeling in my heart that some great enterprise of just this nature was destined to come my way, though little dreaming that the ambition would in fact come true. Just what our great monarch saw in me, or why he placed in my hands the key to such a weighty undertaking, I do not know; but with loving words, which from such lips are a command constraining to more than is asked, he entreated me, saying: "The price of arduous and heroic achievement is toil and fatigue. To risk one's life, even to lose it, is to win renown; for fear is infamous, and the refusal to give way to it, though it may shorten our earthly span, bestows on us the longer life of fame. I have chosen you from among all my people for such an enterprise as is your due. It promises great hardships, but honour and glory as well; and I know that for my sake you will bear all lightly."

'I protested at this, exclaiming: "Your Majesty, to risk sword, fire and extremes of climate for you is so little that I regret rather that my life should be a thing so insignificant. Think of the labours that Eurystheus contrived for Hercules: the Nemean lion, the monstrous harpies, the Erymanthian boar, the fearsome hydra, the descent to the world of shades where the Styx flows through Pluto's domains. All this and more, Your Majesty, I am ready, body and soul, to confront for you."

'The king thanked me, bestowing on me signal marks of his favour and praising loudly my resolve; for valour lauded flourishes the more, and recognition steels men to high adventure. And straightway my dear brother Paulo said he would come with me. The bonds of love and friendship were a part in this, but he was moved no less by the thirst for honour and fame. Nicolao Coelho too joined me, a man of great endurance under hardship and, like my brother, at once prudent and valiant and a fierce and experienced fighter.

'I then set about recruiting my men, choosing youths fired with the spirit of daring and adventure, and indeed those who volunteered proved themselves such by the mere fact of doing so. Manoel appointed them a remuneration calculated to inspire still greater devotion, and heartened them with noble words to endure whatever might befall. The scene resembled the assembling of the Argonauts for the quest of the Golden Fleece, in the search for which their oracular vessel was to be the first, greatly daring, to brave the Black Sea.

'At last, in Lisbon's noble harbour, where the Tagus mingles its fresh water and white sands with those of the salty ocean, the ships lay ready, each imbued with an identical spirit of resolve and exaltation. Crews and fighting men alike were ready to follow me to the ends of the earth, no suspicion of fear tarnishing their youthful ardour. The soldiers came along the strand clad in various styles and colours, and girt about no less with intrepidity for the discovering of new regions of the globe. The wind blew gently, setting the flags with which our stout vessels were bedecked a-fluttering. The Argo ended its days as a constellation in the heavens, and these promised no less when they should have sailed over the infinity of ocean.

'Being now equipped with all things needful for such a voyage, we repaired to Belem Church, named in memory of Christ's birthplace, that stands on the very river-brink, and there disposed our souls against the risk of death that is ever present to seafarers, beseeching God Almighty, on whose holy presence the saints and angels feed, that he should smile on these beginnings and guide our paths. Then, having prayed, we left the church. You may well believe, Your Majesty, that when I recollect how I left my native shores, burdened with doubts and apprehension, I can with difficulty restrain my tears.

'A great concourse of citizens had gathered to see us depart, some our friends and kindred, others mere onlookers. In the faces of all were written grief and dismay as we walked in solemn procession to the ships, accompanied by zealous religious in their hundreds still invoking God's blessing. The crowds looked on us as men already lost, a prey to such far and dubious journeyings. Women wept pityingly, men heaved deep sighs. Mothers, wives and sisters contributed to the chill, despairing fear that it would be many a day before any set eyes on us again, for love knows its own fears that make it the more apprehensive.

' "My son," one woman was saying, "only solace and sweet comfort of my weary old age, that must end now in bitter pain and weeping, why are you leaving me to misery and wretchedness? Why should you go away from me, my dear one, only to perish at sea and be thrown to the fishes?" Another, bare-headed, wailed: "Husband mine, so sweet and dear to me, without whom love has willed that I should find life unbearable, what makes you go risking on the angry waves a life that belongs, not to you, but to me? How can you forget, for so doubtful an enterprise, our so gentle affection? Would you have the wind, as it swells the sails, carry away too the love and the great joy that have been ours?"

'Old men and children, in the manner of their years, accompanied the women in these and the like lamentations of love and pitying tenderness, and the nearby hills made answer as though the same deep grief were theirs. The white sands were drenched with tears equalling their grains in number. We did not dare raise our glance to wife or mother, fearing lest the sight of them so overwrought might unnerve us or shake the firmness of our resolution; and I decided that we should embark without the customary leave-taking, which, though it is the proper usage of love, only grieves the more him who goes and him who stays.

'But there was one old man of venerable aspect among the others on the shore who fixed us with his gaze, shook his head three times disapprovingly and, raising his feeble voice so that from the ships we heard him clearly, drew out of an experienced heart these words of practical wisdom:

' "Oh, the folly of it, this craving for power, this thirsting after the vanity we call fame, this fraudulent pleasure known as honour that thrives on popular esteem! When the vapid soul succumbs to its lure, what a price it exacts, and how justly, in perils, tempests, torments, death itself! It wrecks all peace of soul and body, leads men to forsake and betray their loved ones, subtly yet undeniably consumes estates, kingdoms, empires. Men call it illustrious, and noble, when it merits instead the obloquy of infamy; they call it fame, and sovereign glory, mere names with which the common people delude themselves in their ignorance.

' "To what new disasters is it bent on leading this realm and its people? What perils and deaths has it in store for them, concealed under some fair-sounding name? What facile promises of gold-mines and kingdoms does it hold out to them, of fame and remembrance, of palms and trophies and victories?

' "O unhappy race, true heirs of that madman whose sin and disobedience not only doomed you to gloomy exile from paradise but drove you from that other divine state of simple, tranquil innocence, the golden age, condemning you in its place to this age of iron and instruments of destruction! Now your fickle fancy has become infatuated with this folly that describes as enterprise and valour what is but the cruel ferocity of the brute creation, and boasts of its contempt for life, which should always be held dear if only because he who gives it was so loath to lose his own.

' "Is not the Ishmaelite close at hand, with whom there will always be wars and to spare? If the faith of Christ be the motive, does not he profess the cursed creed of Mahomet? Has not he a thousand cities and territories beyond calculation, if instead lands and riches be the lure? Or, if it be the praises that fall to the conqueror, is not he too a redoubtable antagonist?

' "You allow the enemy to flourish at your gates while

you go seek another at the other side of the world, at the price of depopulating and weakening this ancient kingdom and squandering its resources. You are lured by the perils of the uncertain and the unknown, to the end that fame may exalt and flatter you, proclaiming you with a wealth of titles lords of India, Persia, Arabia and Ethiopia. A curse on him who first launched on the waters a barque with sails! If the faith I follow be true, and I know it is, he deserves to suffer eternally in hell. May he never be renowned or even remembered among those of sound judgement, and may no musician's lyre or poet's imagination ever sing his name. Let rather his name and his fame perish with him!

  ' "Prometheus brought down fire from heaven and, breathing it into the heart of man, set the world ablaze with the clash of arms, dishonour, and destruction. How much better would it not have been for us, Prometheus, and how much less harmful to the world, had you never breathed life into that image of man and fired it with overreaching desires! The luckless Phaethon would then have left Apollo's chariot alone, and Icarus and his father would never have sought to soar through space. A sea commemorates the latter's foolishness, a river the former's. But now there is no undertaking so daring, or so accursed, be it through fire, water, heat, cold or the sword, that man will leave it untried. Wretched in truth is his lot, and strange his nature!"

CANTO

5

'THE worthy old man was still giving voice to these senti-
ments as we spread our sails to the gentle breeze. As they
unfurled we raised a cry, sailor-fashion, wishing ourselves
"Bon voyage", and, the wind setting our ships in motion,
said farewell to the harbour that meant so much to us. It
was the eighth of July of 1497.

'Gradually the hills of our native land faded from sight.
The beloved Tagus lay astern, and the cool heights of
Cintra, on which our eyes lingered fondly. In that dear
homeland we were leaving our hearts behind too, for those
we loved most were there. At length everything was lost
to view, and we gazed only on sea and sky.

'So we ploughed our way through waters where none
save Portuguese had ever sailed before. To our left were
the hills and towns of Morocco, the abode once of the
giant Antaeus; land to our right there was none for certain,
though report spoke of it.

'And now our course took us into regions and past islands
already discovered by the great Prince Henrique. First
came Madeira, so called from its many forests. This was
the earliest of the islands to be settled by Portugal and the
best known to fame. Although set on the very edge of the
known world, none of those beloved by Venus can out-
shine it; had it too been hers she would quickly have for-
gotten Cyprus, Gnido, Paphos, and Cythera.

'Soon we had passed the desert coast of Numidia, where the Senegalese graze their flocks. This is a land that stretches from Barbary to Ethiopia, yet it is entirely lacking in fresh water, and the crops never suffice for sustenance: a land, in short, wholly unfruitful and lacking in all natural resources. The birds there feed on iron.

'We passed the tropic of Cancer, the sun's farthest north, where, thanks to Phaethon, the natives are dark-skinned. They are a strange people, these tribes who dwell by the Senegal River with its chill, dark current. The Cape Arsinarius of the ancients lay here: we call it now Cape Verde.

'The Canaries, known of old as the Fortunate Isles, now lay far behind us, and soon we were sailing among the Hesperides [or Cape Verde Islands], named after the daughters of Hesperis of old, a region with whose marvels our fleets had already become familiar. The wind favouring us, we put in at one of them called Santiago, in memory of the warrior saint who helped the Spaniards to such purpose in their wars against the Moslems. Here we replenished our stores, then, grateful for the refreshment, bade the place farewell, and with a following breeze set sail once more over the mighty ocean.

'We skirted thereafter a large part of Africa, that still lay always to the east: Jalofo, where the Negroes are split into different tribal communities; Mandinga, through whose vast territory the Gambia wends its sinuous way to the Atlantic and where the natives traded gold with us; the Dorcades [or Bissagos Islands], home formerly of the Gorgons, the three sisters with only one eye between them – it was Medusa, not then the ugliest of the three, who once fired Neptune the sea-god with love of her curling tresses, that afterwards, changed into serpents, were to swarm all over the burning sands.

'On past all these we sailed, heading ever to the south: past the forbidding Sierra Leone, past the promontory we call Cape Palmas, on into the mighty Gulf of Guinea. The River Niger too, at whose mouth the sea pounds on shores well known to fame, and where there were already Portuguese settlements, we soon left behind, and with it the famous island of São Thomé, recalling the apostle who put his hand in Jesus's side.

'Then came the mighty kingdom of the Congo, that my countrymen had even then converted to Christianity, with the great Congo River, unknown to antiquity, flowing through it.

'And here at length we crossed the equator, and said good-bye to the familiar constellations of the northern world. In this new southern hemisphere we had already discovered one constellation, the Southern Cross, that before us had never been seen by any. The heavens here sparkle less brilliantly and, having fewer stars, impress less with their beauty. And still we could not tell whether the ocean stretched on for ever or would give way eventually to some other continent. Twice in the year the sun crosses over these regions, giving two summers and two winters in its passage from one to the other extreme. And as we sailed on, now becalmed, now tempest-tossed and sore oppressed, when the angry winds belaboured the waters, we saw the Great and the Little Bear sink into the waves in spite of Juno.

'But even if I had a voice of iron, it would be both wearisome and irrelevant to recount to you at length all the perils that befall and baffle men at sea, the sudden terrifying peals of thunder that threaten to bring the world about one's ears, the lightning-flashes setting the heavens ablaze, the black rainstorms, the dark nights. Men of learning, able through native perception or scientific training to penetrate the hidden secrets of the universe, often reject as mere illusion or misapprehension things that rude mariners, who have known no other school than experience and can only judge by appearances, accept as true. Well, I have seen such things.

'One – I had a clear view of it – was our blessed St Elmo's Fire, that is sometimes to be seen in time of storm and raging winds, when the heavens lower and even strong men give way to tears. And it was no less demonstrably a miracle to all of us, a thing to strike terror to our hearts, to see the clouds drinking up, as through a long spout, the waters of the ocean.

'First a thin smoky vapour formed in the air and began to swirl in the breeze; then out of it there took shape a kind of tube stretching right up to the sky, but so slender that one had to strain one's eyes to see it – made, as it were, of the very stuff of clouds. Gradually it grew and swelled until it was thicker than a masthead, bulging here, narrowing there as it sucked up the water in mighty gulps, and swaying with the ocean swell. At its summit a thick cloud formed, that bellied heavier and heavier with the mass of water it absorbed.

'Sometimes a beast, drinking rashly from an inviting spring, will pick up a leech that fastens on its lip and there sates its thirst with the animal's blood: it sucks and sucks, and swells and swells. In the same way this mighty column waxed ever mightier, and with it the black cloud that crowned it; until at length, sated too, it drew up its lower extremity from the sea and drifted off across the sky, spattering the ocean with its own water returned as rain, restoring to the waves what it had stolen, minus its salty savour. And now let the experts consult their authorities and explain to me if they can these mysteries of nature.

'Had the philosophers of old, who journeyed through so many lands to learn their secrets, witnessed the wonders that I have witnessed as I sailed hither and thither over the waters, what writings would they not have left us, what revelations concerning the workings of the stars in their courses and the many marvels and properties of nature, and every word the naked, unvarnished truth!

'The moon had now passed five times from the crescent to the full since first we put to sea, when one day a keen-eyed sailor shouted from the crow's-nest "Land! Land!" The others rushed on deck in great excitement, scanning the horizon to eastwards. Gradually the hills, vague and confused at first like cloud-shapes, began to reveal themselves. The anchors were got ready, and as we drew inshore the sails were struck. And now, the better to locate our position in these remote parts, we disembarked on a broad expanse of coast where the men were able once more to stretch their limbs, curious to savour the novelties of a land where none had set foot before.

'I meanwhile, with the pilots, stayed by the sandy beach to make my calculations, using that new and ingenious instrument the astrolabe. We took the height of the sun and, studying our charts with the aid of the compass, found that we had now left behind the tropic of Capricorn and were thus heading for that least known region of all, the frozen Antarctic.

'Then suddenly, looking up, I saw my men returning with a black-skinned stranger in their midst, whom they had taken by force as he was gathering honeycombs on the mountain-side. His face betrayed his alarm at finding himself in such a predicament. A savage more uncouth than Polyphemus, he could not understand us, nor we him. I showed him samples of gold, of silver, of spices: they made no impression on him whatever. Then I bade the men produce baubles of no value, glass beads, tiny tinkling bells, a bright red cap; and it was at once clear from his signs and gestures that these delighted him greatly. I told them to let him have the lot and go free, and he made off for his village, that lay not far away.

'Next day his fellows, all naked and black as night, came trooping down from the rugged hill-sides seeking the same for themselves. They seemed so gentle now, and so well-disposed towards us, that Fernão Veloso was emboldened to go back into the bush with them to see their way of life. Veloso had confidence in his own right arm, and believed in his arrogance that he had nothing to fear.

'He was gone for a considerable time, and I was growing anxious for news of him, when of a sudden, scanning the distance, I saw his figure on the hill-side. He was making for the sea, and in somewhat more of a hurry than when he set out. Coelho's skiff made inshore with all speed to take him off; but before it could make the beach a native pounced out on him boldly, to prevent his escaping, and then another, and another. He was in imminent danger, with no one at hand to help.

'I too hastened to the rescue, and while we plied our oars a whole band of Negroes appeared from an ambush, like a black cloud. Soon arrows and stones beyond number began to rain on us, and not all in vain, for it was there I got this injured leg. But we, as the wronged party, did not take it all lying down, and our answer was such that I suspect their caps were not the only red souvenir they had of the incident.

'With Veloso safe in our hands again we at once rowed back to the ships, having had our eyes opened to the ugly malice and savage designs of these brutes. As for India, our goal, all we had learnt from them was that it still lay a very long way off. And so once more we spread our sails to the wind.

'It was then that one of the men said to Veloso, a smile spreading round the company as he spoke: "I say, Veloso, that hill was better for coming down than going up?" "It was that," replied the bold adventurer; "but when I saw so many of those dogs coming this way I hurried a bit, remembering that you were all here without me." And then he told us how, once they had passed the crest, the Negroes would not allow him to go any further, threatening to kill him on the spot if he persisted, and how when he turned back they laid an ambush, thinking to dispatch us as we went to pick him up and so despoil us at their leisure.

'For five days after leaving the spot we sailed on, over seas still uncharted, with a following wind all the time. And then one night as we stood in the prow, watchful but carefree, a cloud appeared overhead, blacking out the sky. It was a monstrous, fearsome thing, and the sight of it filled our hearts with dread. The darkening sea roared from afar, as if battering in vain against a reef. "Heavenly Power," I exclaimed, "what divine threat or what mystery is this that the sea and the elements confront us with, for I am persuaded that it is something more than a storm?"

'I had scarcely spoken when a figure took shape in the air before our gaze. It was of fantastic form and size and powerful build, with a heavy jowl, unkempt beard, and sunken eyes. Its expression was evil and terrifying, its complexion of an earthy pallor. Yellow teeth showed in its cavernous mouth, and its crisp hair was matted with clay. From the size of its limbs it might have passed for a second

Colossus of Rhodes, that was one of the seven wonders of the world.

'And then it spoke, in a mighty, terrifying voice that seemed to come from the depths of the sea. Our flesh went creepy and our hair stood on end as we looked and listened.

' "So, you daring race," it said, "bolder in enterprise than any the world has yet seen, tireless in the waging of cruel wars as in the pursuit of hopeless undertakings: so you have crossed the forbidden portals and presumed to sail on these seas of mine, that I have held and guarded for so long against all comers, whether of these regions or any other. You have come to surprise the hidden secrets of nature and of its watery element, that to no mortal, however great, however noble or immortal his deserts, have yet been revealed.

' "Listen now to me and learn what perils have been laid up against such excess of presumption, what penalties await you over the vast expanse of ocean and on the land that you will eventually subdue in battle. Know that as many ships as are bold to make this voyage that you are making now will be assailed when they reach this spot by hostile winds and raging tempests; and that on the very first fleet to follow you into these untamed waters I shall wreak such sudden chastisement as to make the danger pale before the reality.

' "Here, unless I am deceived, I count on avenging myself to the full on him who discovered me. Nor will the havoc to be visited on your too trusting pertinacity end with this, for every year, if my judgement fail me not, your vessels will suffer shipwreck and catastrophe of every sort, until death shall come to seem the lesser evil.

' "In these waters that illustrious leader whom fame and

fortune are to exalt to the skies as first Viceroy shall meet
his end, for so God in his inscrutable wisdom has decreed:
here he shall lay down the trophies of his victory over the
Turkish fleet. Nor shall the vengeance be mine alone, for
his destruction of Kilwa and Mombasa will likewise cry out
for retribution.

' "Another will come too, one noble, liberal, greatly es-
teemed, and in love, and with him the beauteous lady whose
affections he will have had the rare good fortune to win. A
sorry plight is theirs, and black the fate that brings them
into my realms; for, incensed against them, it will allow
them to survive cruel shipwreck only to vent on them
sufferings still more grievous.

' "They shall see their children, the fruit of so much love,
die of hunger; rough, grasping Kaffirs shall strip the
gracious lady of her garments after a long and painful trek
across the hot sands, leaving her crystal limbs exposed to
all the rigours of the elements. And their fellow-survivors
from so much misery shall see still more: they shall see the
two hapless lovers fall victims of the hot, implacable bush,
where their tears, for the grief that is in them, will melt the
very stones, until after a last close embrace their souls will
take leave of bodies even more wretched than they were
comely."

'The fearsome monster was proceeding with its prophe-
cies of the fates in store for us when I boldly interrupted.
"Who are you," I asked, "for proportions so outrageous
take one's breath away?" It rolled its black eyes, contorted
its mouth and, uttering a giant roar that filled me with
terror, replied in a voice heavy with bitterness, as though
the question were one it would gladly have avoided:

' "I am that mighty hidden cape, called by you Portu-
guese the Cape of Storms, that neither Ptolemy, Pom-

ponius, Strabo, Pliny nor any other of past times ever had knowledge of. This promontory of mine, jutting out towards the South Pole, marks the southern extremity of Africa. Until now it has remained unknown: your daring offends it deeply. Adamastor is my name. I was one of the giant sons of earth, brother to Enceladus, Briareus, and the others. With them I took part in the war against Jupiter, not indeed piling mountain upon mountain but as a sea-captain, disputing with Neptune's squadrons the command of the deep.

' "It was for love of Thetis, Peleus's wife, that I joined in the campaign. I saw her one day come up on to the beach, naked, with the other Nereids, and so lost my heart to her straightway that I still love her as I have never loved another. None of the goddesses on Olympus meant any-thing to me in comparison with that princess of the waves. But there was no hope of winning her affection with features as huge and ugly as mine, so I made up my mind to have her by force, and told her mother so.

' "Doris was terrified, and spoke to Thetis on my behalf; but she only laughed, a modest, comely laugh, and said: 'What love of nymph can match a giant's ardours? Still, if war on the ocean be the alternative, I must do what I can to avert it, provided my good name be not com-promised.' Such was the reply her mother brought back to me. I was slow to suspect deceit – there is none so blind as the man in love – and her words filled me with hope and quickened desire.

' "In my folly I desisted from the struggle against the gods, and one night, as Doris had promised, I saw the fair Thetis coming from afar, her face as lovely as ever and her body still more lovely in its nakedness. Beside myself with joy, I ran with open arms to greet her who was life itself to me, and began to smother her eyes, her hair, her every feature with kisses. Alas! – I scarce know how to tell it, in my anger – when I thought I held my loved one in my arms, I realized that instead I was clasping a rocky cliff bristling with thickets, its summit what had been her angelic face. Nor was I, for the moment, any longer human. Struck dumb and motionless, I might have been a second cliff.

' "Fairest Nymph of ocean, if you could not abide my presence, why did you not transform me for good, whether into a hill-side, a cloud, a dream, or just nothingness? I could not stay on there now: the shame and the ignominy of it infuriated me until I feared I should take leave of my senses. So I set out in search of another world, far from the sight of one who laughed at my tears and my misfortunes.

' "My brothers by this time had been defeated and utterly cast down. Some of them the gods buried underneath mountains, the better to secure their victory. It was clear that mere strength is of no avail against the heavens, and I, left to weep over my woes, began to realize that fate was against me and to feel the weight of its displeasure at what I had dared. My flesh changed to hard earth, my bones to crags. These limbs you see, this frame, were then projected across the vast watery spaces, until finally the gods completed the transformation of my huge bulk into this remote headland. And, to double my sufferings, Thetis still pursues me with these encircling waves."

'Such was his tale, and with a fearsome lament he vanished from before our eyes. The black cloud scattered, and a mighty roar broke from the sea and resounded afar. I raised my hands in supplication to the blessed angels who had watched over us thus far, and prayed God to avert the grim disasters Adamastor had foretold.

'The radiant chariot of the sun was now once more approaching, and we began to discern the cape into which the giant had been transformed. For some little distance we sailed along the coast, our prows now at last heading eastward, and then landed a second time. The inhabitants here were still Negroes, but of a more civilized behaviour than those of our earlier encounter. They came along the sandy beach to meet us, dancing and making merry, and with them their women-folk and fat, sleek flocks that they were driving to pasture. The dusky women rode on the backs of lazy oxen, the most esteemed of all their domestic animals, and sang pastoral songs, rhyming and unrhymed, to the accompaniment of rustic flutes, as did Tityrus long ago.

'They were an easy-going people, and treated us in friendly fashion, bartering with us fowls and sheep for trinkets; but when my men had failed to elicit from them any information concerning the land we sought, we weighed anchor and set sail once more.

'And now, hugging the coast, we had made a great sweep round the south of the Dark Continent and, turning our backs on the South Pole, were heading once again for the equator. Soon we had left behind us the island of Santa Cruz, the farthest point reached by Bartolomeu Dias after his discovery of the Cape of Storms. We sailed on for many days after this, through weather both fair and foul, with only arduous hope now as our guide, for none had sailed this way before us.

'At one time we really were at issue with the sea, creature of change that it is, when we encountered a current so strong that there was no making headway against it. Though the wind was in our favour, it could at first do nothing against the waves, that drove us back relentlessly;

until at length, stung to anger by the challenge, it increased to gale force and carried us triumphantly through.

'On the Feast of Epiphany we made land again, in an anchorage at the mouth of a great river which we called the River of the Kings, in memory of the day. The natives were still of the same race. They gave us some supplies, and from the river we drew fresh water. But apart from this they were most uncommunicative, and concerning India there was no word to be got out of them.

'Consider, Your Majesty, the distance we had travelled now without ever getting away from these uncouth tribes and without ever coming by news or notion of our goal in the East. You may imagine how low our spirits were, how lost we felt as, worn out with hunger and buffeted by tempests, we hazarded our way through strange climes and unknown waters. Wearied with hope so long deferred, and suffering under the strain of unnatural climatic conditions, we were brought to the verge of despair. Our food supplies had gone bad, so that we ate at our peril, and there was no source of comfort to which we could turn even for the illusion of hope.

'Can you believe that, if these men had not been Portuguese, they would ever have remained faithful as they have to their king and to me their leader? Do you think they would not have rebelled against me, if I had tried to resist, and taken to piracy, driven by hunger, rage, and despair? In truth their metal has been well tested, since no trial, however great, has caused them to falter in that unshakable loyalty and obedience which is the crowning quality of the Portuguese.

'Well, we left the river and its friendly anchorage at length and struck out from the coast some way into the open sea. A chill south wind was blowing, though gently, and we did not wish to be caught in the indentation the coast makes there, by Sofala Bay, that is so famous for its gold. But once past this, we headed our ships back to where the breakers were pounding on the shore, not without breathing a prayer to St Nicholas, for between disappointment and apprehension we were nearly at the end of our tether, and very conscious that only some frail planks stood between us and destruction.

'And then at last something did befall us to make our hearts leap. We were now close in to land, with strands and valleys in full view, and a river entering the sea, and there, plying up and down the river, were sailing-vessels. Our joy was great to come at last on a people that knew the art of navigation, and from whom we might count on getting some news of what we sought. And so, indeed, we did.

'They were Negroes too, but apparently they had dealings with some more civilized race, and in their speech an occasional word of Arabic was recognizable. They wore turbans of fine cotton weave, and a loincloth of the same, dyed blue. Thanks to their smattering of Arabic Fernão Martins, who knows the language well, was able to learn from them that ships about the size of ours sailed over that ocean, coming from the east to regions to the south of them and then returning eastward again, to a land where men's skins were white like ours.

'We got great contentment from our encounter with these people, and from the news they gave us much greater. The river we named the River of Good Omen, and on its bank we set up a stone pillar, one of several we had brought with us to mark such spots, dedicating it to the blessed St Raphael who guided Tobias in his search for Gabael. We took the opportunity here to scrape our keels of all the slime and shells and molluscs they pick up in the deep; after our long time at sea they were badly in need of it. The natives meanwhile played friendly hosts to us, hanging about and showing signs of merriment and delight. They were a people wholly without guile.

'And yet the joy we had in that country at the buoying-up of our hopes was not to be unclouded, for Nemesis hastened to counter it by visiting on us a new misfortune. So it is ordained in Heaven, with this harsh and burdensome condition we come into the world: grief will know constancy, but it is in the nature of happiness to be unstable.

'There befell us, in a word, a disease more dread and loathsome than any I have ever known, that proved fatal to many of our men: their bones now lie buried for ever in a strange and foreign land. It attacked first the mouth and gums, leaving them all swollen and distorted, and as the flesh swelled it rotted, in a way that no one who had not seen it would believe. The stench of putrefaction poisoned the air all around. We had no skilled doctor with us, still less a practised surgeon. Those who had the slightest inkling of the art set to, cutting away the poisoned flesh as if it were dead; and well they might, for a man stricken with the disease was as good as a corpse already.

'And so we left them on that unknown shore, left them for ever, the companions who had shared our every adventure and misadventure from the beginning. What an easy thing it is to give the body burial! Any wave of the sea, any hillock in a foreign land, will serve for the bones of the greatest of men, just as it served for these.

'With hope renewed, yet heavy of heart in spite of it, we weighed anchor and sailed ever onward, following the coast in search of some more certain portent. In due course we came to Mozambique, a cruel country the treachery and villainy of whose people will not be unknown to you, and after that to Mombasa, another land of inhospitable and deceitful tribes.

'And so at last God in his mercy brought us here to this secure port of call, where we have found a friendly reception and such treatment as gives health to the living and life itself to the dead. You have afforded us rest, sweet solace and, once more, peace of mind. And now, should you have been listening attentively, you have heard the whole story you asked me to relate.

'What say you, Your Majesty? Do you think history can show any before us who have ventured forth on such a journey? Did the travels of Aeneas take him half so far, or those of the eloquent Ulysses? Has any daring explorer of the ocean deep seen an eighth part of what I, by dint of skill and enterprise, have seen and still hope to see, for all the poetry that may have been written about him?

'Homer, who drank so deeply of the Aonian spring, seven cities contending for the honour of being his birth-place; Virgil, glory of all Italy, the sound of whose divinely stirring lyre, if it soothed the waters of his native Mincio to slumber, caused the Tiber to swell with pride: let them sing the praises of their more than human heroes and exalt their prowess with constant hyperbole, inventing spell-binding Circes, Polyphemuses, sirens whose song lulled the unwary to sleep, dispatching them under sail and oar to Thrace or to the land of the lotus-eaters, causing the pilot to fall overboard and be lost, loosing imaginary winds from bags, invoking love-sick Calypsos and harpies who foul their food, sending them down to the world of shades to hold counsel with the dead. Well may they deck out their empty fables, mere dream-stuff, with ever new refinements. The story I tell is the truth naked and unadorned and admits no comparison with such, for all their grandiloquence.'

The assembled company were still hanging on the Captain's lips, enraptured by his eloquence, when he ended his long recital of high endeavour. The king praised the sublimity of heart of monarchs renowned in so many wars, and praised no less the bravery down the ages, the loyalty and nobility of spirit, of their people. His followers, likewise deeply impressed, began recounting the incidents which had most compelled their admiration, without ever taking their eyes off the travellers from so distant parts. But now the sun was sinking once more to rest, and the king turned back to the shore and went to his royal abode.

How sweet are praise and glory to the doer of great and famous deeds! Your noble strives to leave behind him a name that will equal or surpass that of his distinguished forbears. Emulation of the illustrious achievements of others has called forth a thousand sublime exploits, and praise bestowed on his fellows is a powerful spur and stimulus to him who would be valorous himself. Alexander esteemed less the resounding deeds of prowess of Achilles on the field of battle than the harmonious verse in which Homer sang of them: this alone he extolled, and wished for himself. Miltiades's famous victory over the Persians filled Themistocles with envy, and nothing, he said, so delighted him as to hear his own exploits sung.

And so Vasco da Gama had striven to show that these voyages of old that all the world tells of did not merit such fame and glory as his own, at which heaven and earth alike stood amazed.

Yet it was thanks to Augustus, who held Virgil's muse in such love and esteem and showered honours, gifts and favours on the poet, that the name of Aeneas and the glory of Rome became famous among men. Portugal too has its Scipios, its Caesars, its Alexanders and its Augustuses, but denies them the gifts for lack of which they remain rude and uncultured.

Augustus in the midst of his greatest reverses could still write poems both learned and graceful, as Fulvia will bear witness after Antony abandoned her for Glaphyra. Caesar, in his campaigns for the subjugation of Gaul, did not find war an impediment to letters: with lance in one hand and pen in the other, he rivalled Cicero himself in eloquence. It is known that Scipio was deeply versed in comedy, while Alexander read Homer so assiduously that he seems to have made of him his bedside book.

Never, in short, was there a great warrior of any nation, Roman, Greek, or any other beyond the pale, save only of Portugal, who was not at the same time a man of science and learning. I say it not without shame, for the reason why none among us stands out as a great poet is our lack of esteem for poetry. He who is ignorant of art cannot value it. For this reason, and not for any lack of natural endowment, we have neither Virgils nor Homers; and soon, if we persist in such a course, we shall have no pious Aeneases or fierce Achilles either. And worst of all is the fact that fortune has made us so uncouth, so austere, so unpolished and remiss in things of the mind that many are scarcely interested even that this should be so, or concern themselves at all with such matters.

Let da Gama be grateful to the Muses that they love his country as they do, and have felt constrained in consequence to exalt his name among his fellow-countrymen by celebrating in verse the whole story of his illustrious and martial enterprise. For neither he nor his were on such friendly terms with Calliope or the other Muses of the

Tagus as to make them on that account leave their weaving of cloth of gold to sing his praise.

It is their sisterly love for the Portuguese people and a disinterested pleasure in bestowing due praise on their collective achievement that alone move the kindly nymphs in the matter. And yet no one should be remiss on this account or shrink ever from a readiness for lofty undertakings, for, if not in this way, then in some other he will not fail to reap his due reward.

CANTO
6

THE pagan king was at pains to give the brave seafarers such entertainment as might win him the friendship of the king of Portugal and of so powerful a people. It grieved him that his lot had been cast in a spot so far removed from the fertile lands of Europe, and not rather in the region of the Strait of Gibraltar. He regaled them accordingly, in the best traditions of Malindi, with games, dances, and other festivities day by day, with agreeable fishing expeditions – so Antony was wont to amuse and beguile Cleopatra – and with banquets of fruit, fish, meat, game, and many a strange dish besides.

Da Gama grew conscious that he was prolonging his stay unduly. There was still a vast expanse of ocean to be crossed, the fresh breeze urged him to take on pilots and supplies and be off, and he resolved to stay no longer. As they took leave, their kindly host desired of the Portuguese that there might always be friendship between them, and requested that in their successive voyagings they would make that a regular port of call. He could wish for no higher boon, he said, than to be allowed to place his kingdom and estate at the disposal of men of such worth, and while he lived he would always be ready to serve so excellent a monarch and so great a people with all his resources, even, at need, with his very life.

The Captain made fitting reply, and then, spreading his

sails, set out once more for the lands of the dawn that for so long now had been his goal. This time he had a pilot above suspicion of double-dealing, who straightway showed that he knew his job, and he sailed in consequence with an easier mind than he had known till then. They were launched now on the waters of the Indian Ocean, with their eyes fixed on the cradle of the sun where it rises resplendent in the East.

And now the wicked Bacchus, sore distraught to think the Portuguese should be on the threshold of the good fortune they deserved, was consumed with anger and began to rage and blaspheme. He saw that the rest of the gods were determined to make of Lisbon a second Rome, and that he was powerless to prevent it, for so it had been decreed by a higher and absolute power. In desperation he left Olympus, and came down to earth to seek some remedy for the situation.

It was to the watery court of Neptune, lord of the seas, that he directed his steps, down to the farthest depths of the deep-lofty caverns whither the sea withdraws and whence, at the challenge of the raging winds, it lashes its waves into fury and sends them forth.

There Neptune dwelt, in the company of the blithe Nereids and other deities of the sea, the waters respecting such space as was necessary for their abode. The unplumbed depths revealed sands of fine silver and lofty towers of translucent crystal framed in a spacious setting; and the nearer one drew the less could the eye determine whether what it beheld was in fact crystal or diamond, so dazzlingly did it sparkle and glitter. The doors were of pure gold richly inlaid with seed-pearl and adorned with sumptuous carvings.

On these, for all his anger, Bacchus could not refrain

from feasting his gaze. And first he saw, depicted with a wealth of colour, the confused features of primaeval chaos with a representation of the four elements about their divers functions. Above was fire, sublimely independent of matter and, ever since Prometheus stole it, the source of life to all living things. After it, soaring lightly and invisibly, came air, that found its habitat more readily and left no corner of the world, however hot or cold, unfilled. Earth, disposed in hills and valleys, was clad in green swards and blossoming trees, whence the beasts that inhabited it derived their varied sustenance; while, scattered about the land mass, water was clearly to be perceived, not merely nourishing many a species of fish but supplying the humidity essential to existence.

In another part was represented the war of the gods and giants, with Typhoeus now buried beneath towering Etna, that spouted crackling flames; while elsewhere Neptune could be seen striking the earth and endowing primitive man with the horse, and peace-loving Minerva bestowing as her gift the olive-tree.

But Bacchus's temper did not suffer him to tarry long over these sights, and he pressed on into the royal halls. Neptune had been advised of his coming and stood there by the portal to receive him, with a following of nymphs curious to behold the god of wine thus bend his steps to the realm of water.

'Fear not, Neptune,' he said, 'to admit Bacchus into your domains, for unjust fate displays its power even against the great and the mighty. But before I say more, pray summon the other sea-gods, if you would know the rest of my story. They will learn of new extremes of misfortune, and it is well that all should hear where all are concerned.'

Judging that these words portended something passing

strange, Neptune dispatched Triton forthwith to call the sea-gods from the farthest corners of ocean. He was a tall youth of dark and unprepossessing features, this Triton, proud offspring of Neptune and the revered Amphitrite, and his father's trumpeter and message-bearer.

His hair, that fell to his shoulders, was matted like his beard with slime and dripping water: it clearly did not know what it was to be gently combed. Black mussels had their home there, and could be seen hanging from his locks. As head-dress he wore a huge lobster-shell. Other attire he had none anywhere, that he might be the less impeded when swimming, but his body was covered with hundreds of small marine animals, shrimps and crabs and moss-stained oysters and cockles and snails with their houses on their backs and many another species of shell-fish, that are at their best when the moon is full.

And now he blew a mighty blast on the great twisted shell he bore in his hand, and the sound of it, re-echoing afar, was heard throughout all the seas. The gods, harking to the summons, all made their way towards the palace of him who once raised the walls of Troy, that the Greeks in their fury afterwards destroyed. Father Ocean came with all his sons and daughters, and Nereus, Doris's husband, who by her peopled the sea with nymphs. Proteus the seer came likewise, leaving his flocks of seals to graze on the salty waters, notwithstanding that he already knew what business it was that had brought Bacchus down.

Tethys was there, too, daughter of Uranus and Vesta and Neptune's fair spouse, whose countenance, at once grave and gay, was so beautiful that the sea was becalmed in admiration: her gown of finest weave revealed the crystal form beneath, for so much beauty was not to be hidden. Nor was Amphitrite, lovely as the flowers, one to miss an occasion like this: she came bringing with her the dolphin at whose solicitation she first yielded to Neptune's love. The two goddesses came hand in hand, with little in truth to choose between them, for both had Neptune to husband and the eyes of either, that reduced to vassalage all they beheld, could well outshine the sun itself.

Leucothea, who became a sea-goddess when, as Ino, she fled from the ire of her husband Athamas, was accompanied by her son, a lovely child also numbered among the gods. He came along the strand playing with the attractive shells that abound in the sea, and now and again the fair nymph Panope would throw her arms around his neck. Glaucus, who through eating of the magic herb was changed from man to fish and thence into sea-god, still wept over the ugly spell cast on Scylla, his fair beloved, by Circe just because she had herself fallen in love with him; for passion unrequited can drive to this, and more.

And now all had taken their places in the great hall of the palace, the goddesses on a richly-cushioned dais, the gods on thrones of crystal. The air was redolent with burning ambergris, that product of the deep whose perfume surpasses the finest Arabia can produce. Neptune, seated on a raised throne with Bacchus by his side, extended to all a courteous welcome, and when the initial tumult of greeting had died down Bacchus began to unfold the cause of his distress. His face clouded somewhat and betrayed the depth of his feeling as he spoke, his whole object being to compass the destruction of the Portuguese by stirring up enemies against them.

'O Neptune,' he said, 'monarch by right of the angry seas from pole to pole, who have set a girdle round the peoples of the earth and forbidden them to transgress their appointed bounds; and you, Father Ocean, who envelop the whole world, hemming it in and by just ordinances decreeing that none shall pitch their abode beyond it; and you, gods of the sea, who suffer none of all who sail its waters to commit a wrong within your vast domain without visiting upon him, whoever he may be, exemplary punishment: what remissness is this that has come upon you? Who can it be who has so softened your hearts, that you had rightly steeled against these weak yet daring mortals?

'You have seen how out of their boundless presumption they have already attacked high heaven, how their demented imaginings have led them to challenge the sea with sail and oar. You have seen – we still see every day – examples of their haughty insolence, such that before very long, I fear, we may find them become gods of sea and sky and ourselves reduced to mortals.

'Consider now how a puny race, that takes its name from a vassal of mine, has made itself master of you and me and the whole world beside with its proud and dauntless spirit. See how they plough a path across your waters in a way that not even the great Romans of old ever did, how they trespass upon your realms and set your decrees at naught. When first the Argonauts blazed a trail through your dominions, I still remember how the north winds took offence and resisted with all their companions. If they felt so deeply the wrong done them by that adventurous band, what are you now waiting for, when revenge is so much more your concern, that you do not set about it straightway?

'But I would not have you think, gods, that it was solely for love of you that I came down from the heavens, nor from resentment at the wrong you suffer. It is the wrong done to me too that weighs on me; for great honours that, as you know, I won among men when I conquered the lands of India in the East I now see tarnished by these people.

'Jupiter, in short, and the Fates, who order human affairs as seems best to them, are resolved to confer on these mortals a fame greater than has ever before been won at sea. You may learn from this how they can instigate to wrong-doing even against the gods, for it seems that the least of these people now ranks as high as he who by rights should overtop them all. That is why I left Olympus, in search of some remedy for my griefs, and hoping perchance to find here in your waters the esteem that is no longer mine up yonder.'

He would have spoken further, but could not, for the tears were rolling down his cheeks; and the sight stirred the passions of his listeners, firing their hearts to an anger that would not brook delay, mature reflection or other impediment to action. A message was immediately dispatched to Aeolus, on behalf of Neptune, bidding him loose the countless furies of the conflicting winds and sweep the seas clear of mariners once for all.

Proteus would have liked well to speak his mind first on the business, and everyone gathered that some profound prophecy was shaping there; but so sudden and so great was the excitement that had taken possession of the gods that Tethys indignantly cut him short, shouting: 'Neptune knows what he is about.'

Already Aeolus was freeing the raging winds from their prison and speeding them with provocative words against the brave and spirited Portuguese. Of a sudden the calm sky grew overcast, and the winds, blowing with unparalleled fury, intensified their violence until houses, towers, even mountains were being levelled in their path.

The fleet meanwhile, all unaware of the council taking place in the watery depths, was being gently wafted onward on its long voyage: the sea was tranquil and the crews, though tired, were joyous at heart. It was night, and the men of the first watch were making for bed while those of the second got up.

Still heavy-eyed and only half-awake, they were yawning and leaning every now and then against the yards. Their clothing afforded them but indifferent protection against the chill breezes that were blowing. Still, their eyes were open, if unwillingly, and they rubbed and stretched their limbs. But they had to find some means of keeping awake, and so they fell to telling stories and recounting strange happenings.

'This is a boring stretch,' one remarked. 'How can we pass it better than by telling some pleasant tale that will put sleep to flight?' 'And where will you find a better tale for killing time than one of love?' said Lionardo Ribeiro, whose thoughts were ever those of the constant lover. 'I do not agree,' put in Veloso. 'Soft topics are not for hard times like these. Life at sea is too strenuous for talk of love and suchlike refinements. Let us dwell instead on war and the heat and perils of battle; for I am very much mistaken if there be not grim days ahead of us. I can feel it in my bones.'

The others agreed, and bade Veloso himself tell them a story on the lines he suggested. 'That I will,' he said, 'and with no fear that you will chide me for spinning you a fabulous tale or one of my own invention. And because I want you to learn from it how to perform great and noble deeds, I am going to choose my heroes from among those of our own nation. Have you ever heard of the Twelve of England?

'It was in the time of João I, Pedro's son, after he had pacified the country and secured it against molestation from Castile. In England, that great northern kingdom of perpetual snow, the spirit of discord was sowing its evil tares, that were to redound to the greater glory of our native Portugal.

'It happened one day that a dissension broke out between the noble lords and fair ladies of the English court, that was soon inflamed to anger. It may have been conviction, it may have been merely provocation, but the courtiers, little recking of the consequences of such a bold and serious charge, affirmed – and undertook to bring forward the necessary proof – that the ladies lacked the honour and repute necessary to their station. And if any were to offer to take the ladies' part, they added, with lance and sword, they would meet them either in open combat or in the lists and punish their presumption with infamy, or death itself.

'The ladies, unused to such insults, and unable in their weakness to defend themselves, called on their friends and kinsmen to come to the rescue. But so high-placed and powerful were their enemies that neither kinsmen nor ad-mirers, however fervent, dared rally as in duty bound to their defence.

'With comely tears running down cheeks of alabaster, such as might have engaged in their cause all the gods on Olympus, they then addressed themselves in a body to the Duke of Lancaster, one of the great English nobles, who had earlier fought with the Portuguese against Castile and there experienced at once the valour and great-heartedness of his comrades-in-arms and the favouring destiny that presided over them. He had experienced equally their disposition to the tender emotions when he saw his own daughter so take possession of their great king's heart that he made her his queen.

'Lancaster, unwilling to foment internal strife, was not himself disposed to succour the ladies in their affront. Instead he said to them: "When I was out there pursuing my claim to the throne of Castile, I found in the Portuguese such daring, such nobility, such admirable qualities that, unless I am much mistaken, your cause needs no other champions. Should this be your pleasure, fair wronged ones, I shall send ambassadors on your behalf informing them in discreet and courtly missives of your plaint. I would suggest further that you yourselves reinforce the appeal of your tears by words of love and endearment, for I believe you will find there succour and stout defenders."

'Such was the counsel given them by the Duke, as one versed in these matters. He then gave them the names of a dozen Portuguese stalwarts, that being the number of the ladies, and bade them draw lots for them so that each might be assured of having her own knight. Then, when it was seen which had fallen to whom, each lady wrote in her own strain to her new defender, all wrote collectively to the king of Portugal, and the Duke wrote to king and knights alike.

'When the embassy reached the Portuguese court there was much excitement. The king himself would gladly have been the first to volunteer, had the prestige of majesty permitted it. As for the nobles, they were at one in their fervent desire to be of the number; but there was no luck save for those already nominated by the Duke.

'The king gave orders for a light vessel to be fitted out in the loyal city of Oporto, from which tradition has it that the kingdom takes its name, and the chosen twelve lost no time in seeing to their attire and their horses and equipping themselves with the latest arms and accoutrements, helmets, crests, mottoes and devices, and multi-coloured trappings. Then, taking leave of their monarch, they set sail from the Douro, a compact band wherein none was distinguishable from his fellows in all knightly virtues, skill or valour.

'There was one, however – Magriço, "the lean one", they called him – who first addressed the others thus: "For long, my most brave companions, it has been my desire to see foreign lands and other waters than those of the Douro and the Tagus, to know other peoples and their laws and ways. And now that the opportunity offers, and there being so much in the world to see, I want, if you will allow me, to travel overland alone and join you later in England. Should anything prevent my being there at the appointed time, for God is the ultimate arbiter in all things, my absence will matter little: you will all do your duty on my behalf. But if my intuitions speak true, no rivers, mountains, no, nor envious fortune either, shall prevail against me to keep me from your side."

'With this he embraced his friends and, with their permission, set forth. He journeyed through Leon and Castile, seeing ancient strongholds that in their time had fallen before a Portuguese onslaught, and on through Navarre, where the perilous peaks of the Pyrenees divide Spain from France. At length, after traversing France and seeing its principal sights, he came to Flanders, that great emporium; and there, whether by chance or design, he tarried many days.

'The remaining eleven meanwhile were sailing, an illustrious company, through the chill northern waters. They reached the English coast, that none of them had seen before, and made their way to London, where they were given a festive reception by the Duke and were waited on and made much of by the ladies.

'And now the day appointed for their encounter with the twelve English knights arrived. The king had guaranteed the lists, and as they donned their helmets, greaves, and coats of mail the ladies, seeing them thus resplendent in their armour, rejoiced that their defence should have been entrusted to the martial spirit of the Portuguese. In their rich attire of coloured silks adorned with gold and jewels beyond number that joy found expression.

'But Magriço was still missing, and the lady whose champion he was was garbed in melancholy at having no one to stand up for her that day. The eleven for their part made known their intention of proceeding with the business as had been arranged, and their confidence of winning the day for the ladies even were they not one short but two or three.

'In a magnificent open theatre, surrounded by all his court, the English king took seat. The spectators were ranged in threes and fours in their allotted places. And nowhere from the Tagus to the Bactrus would you have found another twelve to match the English knights who came out against the eleven Portuguese, whether in strength, valour or unshakable resolve. The horses, champing their golden bits and foaming at the mouth, showed their high mettle. The sun's rays glinted on the armour as on crystal or diamond.

'As the contestants were taking up their positions in this uneven and unfair contest of eleven against twelve, suddenly there was a general commotion among the onlookers. Everyone turned to look at the spot where the disturbance was coming from, and saw that it was caused by the entrance of a knight on horseback, accoutred as if ready for combat. The newcomer paid his respects to the king and to the ladies, and then went straight to join the eleven.

'It was the great Magriço himself, and the way in which he embraced his companions showed him to be one who would never let friend of his down, least of all in time of danger. When his lady saw that this was in truth the upholder of her name and reputation her face brightened, and she straightway arrayed herself in a robe of cloth of gold.

'The signal was given, a trumpet-call that fired and impelled to action the spirited hearts on either side. The combatants dug in their spurs, loosened rein, and then, as the horses' hooves struck sparks from the ground and seemed to make the very earth tremble beneath them, lowered their lances. It was a sight to kindle at once exhilaration and dread in the quaking breasts of all who watched.

'Here a rider was projected, rather than fell, from his horse; there rider and horse tumbled heavily together and one heard a groan. One man's weapons, that had been white, turned red; another lashed his horse's flanks with plumes torn from his helmet. Steeds galloped riderless, and riders elsewhere sought vainly for their steeds. For some, life's brief span ended there in the sleep of eternity.

'Those who sought to continue the fight with swords encountered something more than harness, shield, and coat of mail; and when at length two or three of the English knights found themselves outside the lists, English pride was unseated from its throne.

'But I leave it to the spinners of dreams and fables to be prodigal of words, as they are of time, in conjuring up blows and thrusts of cruel and prodigious ferocity. Enough for my story to say that, after many a resounding deed of prowess, the palm of victory fell to the Portuguese, and to the ladies the triumph and the glory.

'The Duke led the twelve victors off to his palace, where they were treated to much merry-making and festivity. Huntsman and cook were kept busy by the fair ladies, so eager were they to regale their liberators with banquets hour after hour and day after day for so long as the call of their beloved country consented to their remaining in England.

'According to the story the great Magriço continued envious to see the world's sights, and did not return home with the others. Being no novice in affairs of arms, he was thus able to render notable service to the Countess of Flanders, in whose defence he slew a Frenchman in open combat, an encounter that brings to memory the names of Torquatus and Corvinus of old. Another of the twelve journeyed into Germany, where he had a fierce battle with a treacherous German who tried to kill him by subterfuge . . .' But here Veloso's listeners interrupted, asking him not to be in such a hurry to leave Magriço, and his victory: the tale of the other's adventure in Germany could wait. And they disposed themselves once more to listen.

Just then the master, who had been observing the state of the weather, blew his whistle. The sailors awakened from their slumbers and hastened from all sides to their stations. The wind was freshening, and the master, ordering the foretopsails to be taken in, bade them all be on the alert; for the appearance of a black cloud seemed to denote that a storm was brewing. Scarcely had the topsails been lowered when, with a sudden fury, it broke.

'Strike the mainsail!' roared the master. 'Hurry, strike!' But the raging winds did not wait for it to be furled. Catching it full on, they ripped it to shreds with a noise that sounded as if the end of the world had come. The vessel heeled over, shipping a vast quantity of water, and the sailors, struck with a sudden panic and confusion, pierced the heavens with their cries. 'Lighten ship!' the master bellowed. 'Everything overboard! All together! Others man the pumps and keep them going, or we shall founder!'

The soldiers hastened to the pumps with a will; but they had barely reached them before the fearsome pitching of the vessel laid them flat on the deck. Three brawny sailors proved unable between them to govern the helm. They tried holding it on both sides with tackle, but their ingenuity was as unavailing as their strength. Had the winds been out to demolish the Tower of Babel itself they could not have raged with a more cruel ferocity. Against the towering seas, as they reared ever higher and higher, the great vessel seemed dwarfed to the stature of a skiff: it was matter for amazement that it still remained afloat.

As for Paulo da Gama's ship, it appeared to be almost wholly under water. Its mainmast had snapped in two, and the crew were calling on him who came to save the world to save them. Coelho, on his, had had the foresight to strike sail before the storm broke, but his men were just as terrified, and their helpless cries just as loud, as those of the others.

The waves were now piling up to the clouds, now opening in yawning gulfs to reveal the inmost depths of angry Neptune's domains. South winds and north winds raged in combat as if bent on shattering the very fabric of creation. The heavens were ablaze with lightning, its flashes illumining the ugly pitch-black night. By distant shores the kingfisher raised its melancholy song, recalling the tears the tempestuous waves had caused Alcyone long ago, and love-sick dolphins sought refuge in their watery caves from the harshness of the elements that even in the deeps of ocean denied them peace.

Never, not even against the fierce and over-weening giants, had Vulcan, who wrought for his stepson Aeneas his gleaming weapons, forged such thunderbolts. Jupiter the Thunderer did not visit such havoc upon the world when he wiped out mankind with a flood, sparing only Deucalion and his wife, who were later to create a new human race from stones. Many a mountain toppled under the waves' frantic onslaught, many an ancient tree was uprooted by the angry fury of the winds. Little had their tough roots thought that they would one day be turned skywards, or the sands of the ocean-bed that the swirling waters above could toss them to the surface.

When da Gama saw himself threatened with destruction so near to the goal of his desire, with the seas now gaping wide open to uncover hell itself, now surging with renewed violence as high as heaven, there seized him a confusion of apprehension and despair. Possibility of human succour there was none, and he invoked instead that heavenly succour to which all things are possible.

'Divine Providence,' he implored, 'fount of mercy, Lord of earth and sea and sky, who didst lead thy chosen people across the Red Sea to safety, didst deliver St Paul from the perils of wave and quicksand, and didst preserve Noah and his sons from the flood when no one else was saved: if we have already come safely through other fearsome dangers, having known our own Scylla and Charybdis, our own shoals and quicksands, our own ill-famed Acroceraunian rocks, why after so many travails dost thou now forsake us, if this our undertaking offend thee not, to whose glory alone it is directed? Happy they who met their end at the point of an African lance while fighting valiantly for the faith on Mauritanian shores, who left great deeds and shining memories behind them, winning life in the losing of it and by the manner of their dying robbing death of its sting!'

And still, like a stampede of wild bulls, the winds raged and roared, whistling through the shrouds and lashing the storm into ever greater fury. Thunder and lightning gave no respite, their fearsome play threatening to bring the heavens in collapse about the earth, so fiercely did the elements war with one another.

At last Venus, the morning star, at whose approach Orion the sword-bearer takes to flight, was seen twinkling on the horizon, presaging the sun and the bright light of day, and the sight spread joy over sea and land. And up on Olympus its parent goddess beheld the sea, and on it the fleet so dear to her, and was seized at once with fear and anger.

'This, beyond a doubt, is the doing of Bacchus,' she said; 'but he will not be allowed to go through with it, now that I know what he is capable of.' Losing not a moment, she again hastened down to ocean, bidding her amorous nymphs meantime garland their brows with roses. Their auburn tresses called for chaplets of many a hue, and in the result the flowers seemed to have blossomed of themselves on a ground of natural gold of the love-god's own weaving. Her plan was to soften by amorous beguilement this troublesome confederacy of the winds, letting them behold the charms of her beloved nymphs, whose coming surpassed the stars in beauty.

It worked: for no sooner had they come in sight than the vigour with which the winds had till then been waging combat forsook them, and they tendered obeisance as though beaten in the fight. Soon the nymphs had them bound hand and foot with those same tresses that out-sparkled the sun's rays.

The most fair Orithyia addressed herself to Boreas, the one she was fondest of at heart: 'Do not imagine, cruel Boreas, that I am taken in by your protestations of constancy in love; for gentleness is the surest pledge of love, and in the constant lover fury has no place. So take heed. If you do not check instantly this outrageous folly, do not look to me to love you ever again. Instead I shall dread you, for you make my love turn to fear.'

Beauteous Galatea spoke in the same strain to Notus, knowing well that he had long delighted in the sight of her and confident that she could do with him what she would. Notus for his part felt his heart leap within him as though it would burst, doubtful whether such happiness were really to be believed; and in his joy at being asked a lover's favour it seemed a trifling thing that he should abate his turbulence.

The other nymphs wrought a similar sudden change in their respective adorers, and soon, all wrath and fury spent, the surrender to lovely Venus was complete. She promised them as true lovers that their affection would always be reciprocated, and made them swear on her fair hands an oath of homage binding them to loyalty while this voyage should last.

And now bright day was breaking over the hills through which the Ganges pursued its murmuring way; and up aloft, in the crow's-nest, the look-outs suddenly spied land straight ahead. The storm was over, the perils of the outward journey lay behind them, and empty fear took wing.

The pilot from Malindi spoke cheerily: 'This, if I be not mistaken, is Calicut. India at last, the land you have been looking for! And, provided your ambition stretches no farther afield, here your long travails come to an end.'

Da Gama could suffer him to speak no more. Overcome with joy at hearing him recognize the land ahead, he fell on his knees and, raising his hands to Heaven, gave thanks to God for his great mercy. And well he might, to him who had not only guided him to his destination after such toils and fears, but had so suddenly delivered him from the watery grave that the raging winds had contrived for him, so that he still felt like one awakened from a ghastly dream.

It is through just such dire hazards, just such grievous toils and fears, that those who love fame achieve immortal honour and the highest esteem. Not for them the everlasting reliance on their ancient pedigree, the sloth of gilded couch and Russian sable, of novel and dainty dishes, idle strolls, and the endless delights that enervate the noble breast. Not for them the constant indulging of appetites pampered by a fortune that will not suffer its favourite ever to change course or to embark on some heroic and virtuous action.

Their goal is such honours as their stout right arm may win them and they may justly call their own. Ever on guard, girt with tempered steel, exposed to storms and tempestuous seas, overcoming the numbing cold of far southern climes and regions bereft of natural protection, subsisting on rations gone putrid with as only seasoning rigours and hardships, compelling a confident, cheerful, and resolute countenance when the cheek pales at the searing whistle of a cannon-ball that carries off a comrade's arm or leg: it is thus that there is bred in the human breast a callous, ennobling contempt for honours and wealth, the honours and wealth that come by fortune's whim and not as the reward of virtue and endurance. It is thus that, with understanding deepened and matured by experience, there are revealed to one, as from a commanding eminence, all the pettiness and futility of ordinary life.

Such a one, in a society ruled by justice and not personal interest, will make his way to the top, as is his due, without seeking to and even against his will.

CANTO

7

AND now land was close at hand, the land so many others had longed to reach, that lay between the Ganges, sprung from the earthly paradise, and the Indus. Take courage, my brave men, who have set your hearts on the victor's palm. You have arrived: the land of wealth abounding lies before you.

You are a very small part of mankind, you Lusitanians, a very small part even of God's fold; and yet neither peril, nor self-seeking, nor lukewarmness in devotion to Mother Church deters you from the conquest of the lands of the infidel. As few in numbers as you are stout of heart, you do not pause to reckon up your weakness. Facing death in manifold forms, you spread the faith that brings life eternal; for Heaven has willed that, few though you may be, you shall do great things for Christendom. So high, O Lord, dost thou exalt the humble!

Consider the Germans, that far-flung and headstrong people who are even now in revolt against the successor of St Peter and have set themselves up a new shepherd and a new creed. And, not content with the blindness of their ways, they are engaged in unworthy strife, not against the overbearing Turk, but against the Emperor, whose yoke they seek to throw off.

Look at the dour English king, calling himself Lord of Jerusalem, that ancient and most holy city that is now in

Moslem hands. If ever a title was at odds with the truth, this is it. He disports himself amid his northern snows fashioning his own brand of Christianity, his sword unsheathed, if at all, not for the recovery of the Holy Land but in persecution of the true followers of Christ. And so, while he disregards the sacred law of the Heavenly Jerusalem, an infidel monarch denies him possession of the one on earth.

And what shall I say of you, unworthy Frenchman, who sought for yourself the title of 'Most Christian'? It was not with any thought of defending the name, or even of respecting it, that you wished it; your actions have instead offended and debased it. You advance claims to the territories of other Christian rulers, as if your own were not large enough. Why not to those of Barbary and Egypt, where the name of Christian is held in enmity? It is there, against such as would reject the very corner-stone of the Church, the supremacy of Rome, that the valiant should draw the sword. From Charlemagne and St Louis you inherited title and estate; did you not inherit too the motives they had for waging just war?

And what of those who, grown forgetful of the valour of their ancestors, waste their lives in the pursuit of wealth and the pleasures of shameful indolence while tyranny sows dissension among a once brave people that is become its own worst enemy? It is with you, Italy, I speak, sunk in a welter of vices and divided against yourself.

O wretched Christians, are you perchance but the dragon's teeth that Cadmus sowed, that you thus deal death one to another, being all sprung from a common womb? Do you not see the Holy Sepulchre in the possession of dogs of infidels who, strong in their unity, are advancing even against your own native soil and covering themselves with glory in the field? You know that with them it is both custom and obligation – and of this injunction they are meticulous observers – to hold their restless forces together by waging war on Christian peoples; while among you the Furies never weary of sowing their hateful tares. Take note then, in case you may have lulled yourselves into a sense of security, that you have two enemies, yourselves and them.

If it be the lust for empire that makes you attempt the conquest of lands not your own, have you forgotten the Pactolus and the Hermes with their gold-bearing sands? In Lydia and Assyria they weave with thread of gold. There are gleaming veins of the metal to be discovered in Africa. Should the very abode of Christ on earth leave you unmoved, surely you can at least be stirred by so great riches.

These fearsome new inventions of guns and artillery, why have they not been tried out before now on the walls of Byzantium and Turkey? The Turks are interfering more and more in the affairs and the wealth of this Europe of yours: why do you not drive them back to their primitive caves in the Caspian hills and amid the arid rigours of Scythia? Greeks, Thracians, Armenians, Georgians alike are crying out to you against the harsh tribute laid on them by this brutal race, which at the blasphemous behest of the Koran carries off their beloved children. It is on the chastising of such inhuman practices as these that you should base your reputation for bravery and skill in war, and not on arrogant boasting of your prowess in fighting one another.

Madmen that you are, thirsting in your blindness for the blood of your own! But here at least, in this small land of Portugal, there will not lack those who will do and dare for Christendom. In Africa they already hold coastal bases;

in Asia none can dispute their sovereignty; in the New World they are ploughing the fields. Were there more lands still to discover they would be there too.

But let us see what is happening to our famous navigators, now that Venus has calmed the blustering fury of the hostile winds and they are come at last in sight of land, the goal of their so constant perseverance, the land to which they have come to spread the faith of Christ, bringing to its peoples a new way of life under a new sovereign.

As they drew in to the strange shore they came upon small fishing-smacks hailing from Calicut. These told them how to get there, and to Calicut accordingly they set their course; for among all the fine cities of Malabar this was the finest, as well as being the seat of the king who ruled over the whole land.

Beyond the Indus, lying between it and the Ganges, there extends a vast territory, not unknown to fame, whose southern boundaries reach to the sea and whose northern to the cavernous Himalayas. Divers kings rule over it, and there are in consequence divers religions: some worship the infidel Mahomet, some bow down to idols, others to native animals. And in that mighty Himalayan range that divides a whole continent – for it stretches right across Asia, taking different names in different regions – are to be found the sources of these rivers which empty their huge volume into the Indian Ocean, embracing the entire land, peninsula-wise, in their course.

To the south the country is shaped in the form approximately of a pyramid, ending in a point that reaches the sea over against the island of Ceylon.

Not far from the source of the Ganges, according to ancient report, there dwelt a people who lived by inhaling the perfume of flowers. Today the names and customs of the inhabitants have changed and multiplied. There are the people of Delhi and the Pathans – these two are the most numerous and hold the greatest territories – those of the Deccan and of Orissa, who pin their hope of salvation on the murmuring waters of the Ganges, and the Bengalis, with the fertility of whose soil no other can compare. There is the warlike kingdom of Cambay – it was here, they say, that the great king Porus ruled – and the kingdom of Narsinga, more notable for its gold and precious stones than for the valour of its people.

Here, over towards the sea, there is a lofty mountain range stretching for a considerable distance that serves as bastion to Malabar against attack from Canara. The natives speak of it as the Ghats. At its foot there runs for some little way a narrow coastal strip buffeted by the ocean breakers, and it is on this that Calicut stands, a rich and beautiful city and unchallenged capital of the empire. Its lord is known as the Samorin.

As soon as the fleet had reached this seat of wealth and power, one of the Portuguese was sent ashore to inform the pagan ruler of their arrival from such distant parts. The messenger made his way up the river-mouth, and the strangeness of his aspect – for everything about him, colour, features, clothes, was new – straightway drew the whole population to see the sight.

Among the crowd was a Moslem born in Barbary, where the giant Antaeus once held sway, and there, before fate bore him to such distant exile, he had either had occasion to visit the neighbouring kingdom of Portugal or had made the acquaintance of its people in battle. At sight of the messenger his face brightened, and, speaking in Spanish, he hailed him with a 'And who brought you to this other world, so far from your native Portugal?'

'We have come across the mighty deep,' the other replied, 'where none has ever sailed before us, in search of the Indus. Our purpose is to spread the Christian faith.' The Moor, Monsaide by name, listened as the other told him of the long voyage and the many perils that had attended it and was filled with amazement.

When the Portuguese intimated at length that the true significance of his tidings was for the king's ear alone, Monsaide informed him that the king's palace lay outside the town, though only a little distance, and that it would take some time for word of this so unexpected embassy to reach him. He suggested that meanwhile he might care to accept the hospitality of his own humble abode and partake of such fare as the land provided. Then, when he had rested a little, he would accompany him back to the fleet, for there is no joy comparable to that of meeting near neighbours in an alien land.

The Portuguese gladly accepted this offer from the jubilant Monsaide, and ate and drank with him and listened to what he had to tell him as if they had been old friends. Then together they went back to the ships, whose lines were so familiar to the Moor, and boarded the flagship, where he got a kindly welcome from everyone. The Captain embraced him, overjoyed to hear again the clear Castilian speech, then sat him next to him and, all attention, plied him with questions about the land and its ways, the sailors crowding round to listen as the trees once did in Rhodope, drawn by the strains of Orpheus's golden lyre.

Monsaide began: 'Dear neighbours, for so nature made my native land and yours, tell me what great destiny or stroke of fortune led you to embark on such a journey. Some deep-hidden reason there must have been to make you leave the Tagus and the Minho, rivers that no one here has ever heard of, and sail across uncharted seas to these remote and out-of-the-way regions. It can only be God who brought you, for some end of his own that he would have you achieve. Otherwise there would be no explaining his guiding you and protecting you alike from enemies and from the raging sea and angry winds.

'You must know that you are now in India, the abode of a diversity of peoples who prosper and grow rich on their gleaming gold and precious stones, their cinnamon and spices. This country where you have now made harbour is called Malabar. Its people worship idols, as did their fathers before them: it is a cult widespread in these parts. They have a number of different kings, though according to tradition there was once one only. Sarama Perimal was the name of the last to hold single sway over the whole territory.

'It was in his time that there came here other peoples from the region of the Red Sea, bringing with them the worship of Mahomet, the same in which I was brought up. Through the eloquence and learning of their preachers they converted Perimal, who adopted their faith with such fervour that he formed the resolve to die a fakir. To this end he fitted out ships, loaded them with a careful selection of merchandise, and embarked for Medina, the last resting-place of the Prophet, there to lead a life of devotion.

'But first, as he had no direct heir, he divided up his kingdom and power among his people, choosing those who were most dear to him and raising them from poverty to riches and from subservience to freedom. On one he be-stowed Cochin, on another Cananor, on others again Chale and Pepper Island and Quilon and Cranganor and the other territories, in accordance with the past services and the merits of each.

'One youth, much loved by him, presented himself too late for a share in the distribution. Only Calicut remained, a city already famous and wealthy through its trade; so this he gave him, and with it the exalted title of Emperor, thus setting him over the others. Then, having settled his affairs, he set out with all diligence for Arabia, there to live and die in sanctity. And hence the title of Samorin borne by the youth and his descendants, giving them precedence and power over all other rulers; and the present emperor is of his line.

'The people here, rich and poor alike, are of the one religion, which is full of lies and superstition. Apart from a loincloth they wear no clothes. There are two castes, an upper and more ancient one called Naires, and a lower, the Pariahs, who are forbidden by their creed to intermarry with the others. Craftsmen can marry only within their craft and the children must follow the same calling, which they are never allowed to change. The Naires hold it a great defilement to be even touched by a Pariah; and if this should ever happen they cleanse and purify themselves with infinite ceremony, just like the Jews with the Samaritans of old.

'You will see much more that is strange in this country, with its great variety of customs. The profession of arms is reserved to the Naires, who are alone privileged to defend their king against his enemies: they wear a shield on the left arm and in the right carry a sword.

'Their priests are Brahmins, an ancient and venerable title; their precepts those made famous by Pythagoras, who first gave philosophy its name. Thus they never kill any animal, and abstain rigorously from the eating of flesh, as if afraid to. It is only in matters of love that they show a greater licence and lack of self-control, wives being held in common within the husband's caste. Happy the lot, and happy the people, where jealousy is no ground for taking offence!

'These customs and many another are practised by the Malabaris. As for the country, it is bursting with merchandise of every kind, thanks to its maritime traffic with other lands from China to the Nile.'

While the Moor was telling all this, the report of the strangers' arrival was spreading through the city, and now the king sent some of his nobles to know the truth of it all. These were already making their way through the streets, surrounded by young and old of both sexes, in search of the Captain of the fleet.

Having received the royal permission to disembark, da Gama lost no more time in making for the shore. He was richly clad, and accompanied by a noble band of Portuguese; and as they rowed slowly across the stretch of sea and then up the estuary the colour and engaging variety of their attire filled the townspeople with delight.

On shore, surrounded by Naires, stood one of the high officials of the realm, known in their language as Catual, who awaited da Gama's arrival with an air of unwonted festivity. As he stepped ashore the Catual embraced him and led him to a luxuriously appointed palanquin, this, carried on the shoulders of bearers, being their customary mode of travel.

And so, the Portuguese in one, the Malabari in another, they set out for the king's residence. The other Portuguese followed on foot, marching in ranks like a squad of infantry. There was much puzzlement in the faces of the onlookers at the strange sight, and they would have liked well to question the foreigners, had not the Tower of Babel made that impossible long before.

Da Gama and the Catual meantime carried on a desultory conversation, Monsaide interpreting as much as he understood of the two languages; and so they progressed through the city until they came to an impressive temple, into which they both entered. Within were images of the gods of the country, carved in wood and stone with a variety of faces and colourings, being so many imaginings prompted by the devil.

The statues were abominable, resembling the chimera that was part lion, part goat, part dragon. To Christian eyes accustomed to representations of God in human form it was an astonishing spectacle. One god was depicted with horns springing from his head, like the Libyan Jupiter Ammon; another had two heads, like Janus of old; a third, with a great number of branching arms, suggested an imitation of Briareus; a fourth had the head of a dog, recalling the Anubis of Memphis.

Here the barbarous heathen performed his superstitious devotions, and both then made their way to the royal palace without further deviation. The concourse of onlookers was constantly swollen with new arrivals anxious to see the foreigner; roofs and windows were festooned with old men and boys, women and girls.

The bearers moved quickly, and soon they drew near to the lovely, fragrant gardens that concealed the royal abode from view, for the magnificence of this did not reside in lofty towers. The noble buildings were set in the midst of delightful groves, so that the monarch lived at once in the country and in the city.

In the wall surrounding the demesne were gateways that bore witness to the architect's skill, with their figures drawn from remotest antiquity to illustrate the nobility of India. So lifelike were the representations of events from those ancient times that the informed observer could clearly recognize the substance in the shadow.

One depicted a mighty army marching along the banks of the Hydaspes. In command was a general with carefree brow, his weapon a staff twined about with vine-shoots and ivy. It was he who built the city of Nysa by the same flowing river, and so true was the likeness that, had Semele been there, she would have said for a certainty that this was her own son Bacchus.

Farther on, a great multitude of Assyrians were drinking the river dry, their leader Semiramis, a woman as beautiful as she was unchaste. Close by her side, that never lacked company, was carved a fierce and ardent steed, whose place her own son was later to dispute, so criminal was her passion, so barbarous her incontinence.

On still another there waved the glorious banners of Greece, which subdued the land as far as the waters of the Ganges, so creating the third empire of ancient India. At their head was the youthful Alexander, decked with the palms of victory and already proclaiming himself the exalted offspring, not of Philip of Macedon, but of Jupiter himself.

As the Portuguese were studying these memorials, the Catual addressed da Gama, saying: 'The time will come, and soon, when other victories shall cast into the shade those you see here recorded. New chapters of history still remain to be written by other foreign peoples who have yet to reach these shores. So much was clear to our sages and seers when they peered into the future. And the magic science has told them this too, that against the might of these newcomers no human resistance can prevail, for there is nothing man can do against destiny; adding, however, that such will be the martial qualities of these strangers, in war and in peace, that to the ends of the earth it will be accounted glory to the vanquished to have such victors.'

But now they were already entering the room where, on a couch unique in the richness and delicacy of its workmanship, the head of that great empire lay reclining. His expression in repose was that of a venerable and prosperous ruler; his robe was of cloth of gold, and on his brow was a diadem of precious stones. By his side an old man knelt reverently and from time to time handed him betel-leaves, which he chewed after the Indian manner.

A Brahmin of high rank stepped softly forward to present da Gama to the king, who motioned to him to be seated in front of him. He sat down by the royal couch, his companions standing some little distance away, and the Samorin's gaze was quick to scrutinize the garb and appearance of men such as he had never seen before.

Then the Captain spoke, his voice welling up resonantly from a breast full of wisdom, so that the king and all his attendants were straightway impressed with the weight of its authority. 'A great king in the West,' he said, 'in the regions where the revolving heavens cause one half of the earth's surface to plunge the other into gloom, denying it the light of the sun, has heard the report, which echo has carried so far afield, that the overlordship and majesty of all India are vested in you, and wishes to be bound to you in friendship.

'He sends accordingly, by long and devious journeyings, to inform you that his own kingdom abounds in all the wealth to be found on land or sea from the Tagus to the Nile and from the chill shores of Holland to the equator, where the sun, beating down on the people of Ethiopia, makes day and night of equal length.

'Should you be willing, by means of pacts and treaties of peace and friendship contracted in all sanctity and sincerity, to allow an interchange of trade between the products of your land and of his, whereby the wealth and plenty of both kingdoms may increase – and there is no greater incentive to a people's industry – it will of a certainty redound to your benefit, as it will bring much glory to him.

'And to the end that the bond of such friendship between you may never weaken, he will be prepared, so often as your kingdom may be endangered by war, to hasten to your defence with men, arms and ships in such a manner as brother would to brother. And he would have you give me a forthright answer as to your feeling in the matter.'

Such was the Captain's message. To it the heathen ruler made answer that it was a great honour to him to receive ambassadors from so distant a nation; but that concerning the proposal he would not take a final decision until after consultation with his ministers, informing himself first with certainty about the king, the land, and the people of whom he had spoken. The Captain might rest meantime after his arduous experiences; he for his part would resolve shortly as the communication deserved, and so enable him to carry back to his sovereign a heartening reply.

And now night was setting its customary term to men's weariness, that their tired limbs might find refreshment in gentle sleep and their eyes relax in forgetfulness. Da Gama and his compatriots were given hospitable lodging in the royal palace, amid much festivity and general rejoicing.

The Catual, diligent as ever in his master's service, had already been charged to learn all he could about the foreigners, where they came from, what their land was like, and the nature of their customs and religion.

As soon, therefore, as he saw Apollo's fiery chariot bring in a new day, he sent for Monsaide that he might sound him concerning them, and enquired of him with eager curiosity whether he could vouch with full knowledge for their nationality, for he had heard that they came from a country very near to the Moor's own native land. He urged him in the royal interest to give the fullest and most detailed information he could, that the king might know what it were best he should do in this business.

Monsaide replied: 'Much as I should like to tell you more concerning these people, I cannot. All I know is that they come from a land on the farther side of Spain, where the sun sinks to rest in the same sea that washes my native shores; and that in religion they follow a Prophet born of a Virgin by the Holy Ghost, as was decreed by the God who rules the universe.

'What was common knowledge among my forefathers concerning them is the fame of their valour and prowess in war. This they themselves experienced to their cost when, in a succession of memorable exploits achieved by more than human bravery, the Portuguese expelled them from the fertile banks of the Tagus and the Guadiana. And not content even with that, they have pursued my people across the tempestuous seas into Africa, where they will not let us live in peace, but seize our cities and fortresses.

'In whatever other wars they have been engaged, whether with the warlike peoples of Spain or with enemies who have come down from the Pyrenees, they have proved themselves no less formidable and resourceful. In short, they are not known ever to have acknowledged defeat. You may take my word for it that no one has yet played Marcellus to these Hannibals.

'Should there be anything further you wish to know, ask

them, for they are a truth-loving people whom nothing annoys or offends like falsehood. Go and see their ships, their weapons, their artillery that nothing can stand up to: you will find the Portuguese way of life, alike in peace and in war, full of interest.'

The pagan was consumed with desire to see these things the Moor had spoken of, and gave orders for boats to be got ready that he might go out and inspect the vessels. The two then put off from the shore together, followed by Naires in such numbers that the sea was solid with their craft.

Climbing on board the impressive flagship, they were received by Paulo da Gama beneath purple awnings, with banners of rich silk all around. On these were depicted warlike deeds from the past, hazardous battles, fierce duels and the like fearsome scenes, that immediately caught and held the Catual's gaze, and he asked for them to be explained to him.

Paulo bade him first be seated and partake of refreshment, and wine was poured; but the other, on grounds of religious scruple, would neither eat nor drink. Suddenly the air was rent with a trumpet-call, such as in time of peace can still evoke the image of war. Cannon thundered, and the diabolical explosion re-echoed to the bottom of the sea.

The heathen took note of all this, but it was plain that his attention was still riveted on the singular exploits summarily represented in the paintings. He rose and, with da Gama on one side and Coelho and the Moor on the other, fixed his eyes on the martial portrait of a white-haired old man of venerable aspect, one whose name can never die so long as men continue to live in society. His dress was wholly Greek, and in his right hand he bore as insignia a branch.

He had a branch in his hand . . .

But what blindness, what rash folly, ye Nymphs of the Tagus and the Mondego, is this, that I should embark on an undertaking so arduous, so long, and so varied without your aid! I invoke your favour, for I am sailing now on the high sea with such a contrary wind that, should you help me not, I greatly fear my frail barque must founder.

Consider for how long now, while I have been celebrating in song your Tagus and your Portuguese, fortune has kept me on my travels, confronted with ever new trials and perils, now tempest-tossed at sea, now exposed to the inhuman hazards of war, another Canace self-condemned to death with the sword in one hand and a pen in the other.

I have known exile under alien roofs with hateful poverty for a companion. I have been raised up by hope, only to be cast down again to still lower depths. I have escaped shipwreck with my life hanging on a thread so slender that Hezekiah, king of Judah, did not cheat death more miraculously.

And still, O Nymphs, it was not enough that I should be hounded by such an enormity of woes. It remained for me to see my verses rewarded as they were by those whose deeds I sang. Where I had looked for leisure and laurel wreaths, they found me instead new refinements of toil and condemned me to an existence harsher than before.

Reflect, Nymphs, on what a breed of stalwarts it is your Tagus nurtures, that are incapable of higher esteem than this, or other favours, for him who gives them glory through his song. What an example is theirs to future writers, what a stimulus to enquiring minds to record for posterity deeds deserving of eternal fame!

In the midst of such ills it is imperative that your bounty at least shall not fail me, and never more than now, when I must exalt a succession of heroic incidents. Withhold it not, I pray you: of you alone I ask it, as one who has already sworn never to employ it where it is undeserved, nor to praise for flattery's sake the merely eminent. May I never myself meet gratitude if I do.

And do not think either, Nymphs, that I would bestow fame on such as place self-interest before the common good and that of their king, in violation of the laws of God and man. He shall not be sung by me who is ambitious to achieve high office to the end simply that he may the more fully indulge his vices by unworthy means; nor he who uses power to pursue his own base desires and who, to catch the shifting favour of the populace, will cut more figures than ever Proteus assumed.

Fear not, Muses, that I shall sing the grave and honest-seeming man who accepts office at his monarch's instance, only thereafter to rob and despoil the poor; nor the man who holds it right and just that royal decrees should be observed with all severity, yet will admit neither the fairness nor the considerateness of paying the worker for the sweat of his brow; nor him who, lacking a fund of experience, would base a claim to prudence on the ingenuity of his grounds for taxing with greedy rapacity the labours of others, from which he stands aside.

They alone shall be my theme who for God and king adventured life itself and, losing it, won a larger life in the fame their works have so richly merited. Apollo and the Muses have accompanied me thus far: I look to them for redoubled inspiration when, having rested, I take breath and return to my task refreshed.

CANTO

8

THE Catual stood before the first of the painted figures,
the one with the long, white, well-combed hair and the
symbolic branch in his hand. 'Who was he,' he asked, 'and
what is the meaning of this symbol he is holding?' Paulo
replied, the knowledgeable Moor again acting as inter-
preter: 'All these figures you see here, of so brave and
martial aspect, are known to fame as having been much
graver and more redoubtable still in their lives and ex-
ploits. They belong to bygone ages, but their names live on
resplendent among those of the outstandingly great.

'The one you are looking at now is Lusus, from whom,
tradition has it, our kingdom of Lusitania derives its name.
He was son and companion to Bacchus, whose conquests
took him to so many parts of the world; and it seems that in
his unwearying devotion to arms he came at length to
Spain and Portugal, where, in the luxuriant plain that lies
between the Douro and the Guadiana, once called the
Elysian Fields, he found such contentment as made him
choose there to lay his weary bones to eternal rest, and in so
doing to give our people a name. The green branch you see
him carry as a token is the thyrsus, the same that Bacchus
used: it is the sign to our times of the relationship that
bound them.

'This other who has just completed a long sea voyage
and whom you see here by the banks of the Tagus is

Ulysses. He is engaged in building city walls that are destined to outlast time itself, as well as a temple to Minerva of which men still speak. It was Minerva who gave him the gift of eloquence: hence the temple. In Asia he set fire to the famous city of Troy; here in Europe he is founding the mighty city of Lisbon.'

'And who is this who is strewing the battlefield with corpses in his fury?' asked the heathen. 'He has defeated whole armies, with eagles painted on their standards.' 'His name,' said Paulo, 'was Viriato. At first he was a mere shepherd tending his flocks. But he proved more skilled with the lance than with his crook, and lived to strike a heavy blow at the prestige of Rome. An invincible warrior he was, and rightly famous. The Romans did not behave to him with the chivalry they showed to Pyrrhus: they could not afford to. He terrified them, and, unable to defeat him by force, they compassed his death by shameful subterfuge. For a nation may be honourable and yet be driven on occasion by dire exigency to break the laws of magnanimous conduct.

'And here is one who was so incensed against his country, that had exiled him, that he threw in his lot with the Lusitanians. He chose well, for in joining them in their revolt he won for himself undying fame. With them he too won victories over the Roman eagle, for even in those early days the most warlike peoples suffered defeat at our hands. Observe how astute and deceptive was his method of persuading towns to come over to his side: a pet hind gifted, he said, with the power of prophecy, that acted as his counsellor. He is Sertorius, and the hind is his heraldic device.

'And now look at this banner, which portrays Dom Henrique, the great progenitor of our earliest kings. We hold him to have been a Hungarian, though foreigners say he was born in Lorraine. In the war against the Moslems he cast the knights of Galicia and Leon into the shade, and then he went to the Holy Land, for he was a saintly man and wished thereby to sanctify the new dynasty.'

'And who, tell me, is this other figure I find so frightening,' asked the Malabari, astonished anew, 'who with so few followers has routed and destroyed so many armies, razed so many bastions, fought indefatigably so many battles, trampled crowns and standards underfoot in so many places?'

Paulo told him. 'That is Afonso I, who won back all Portugal from the Moslem, and because of whom Fame has sworn by the waters of the Styx to stop celebrating the heroes of Rome. For his great zeal he was beloved of God, who used his valour to subdue the infidel foe and gave him his reward in the levelling of all their strongholds, so that nothing remained for his successors to do. Had Caesar or Alexander had so little resources and so few men against enemies as numerous as this great leader vanquished, you may well believe that their names would never have reached so far nor lived so long. But enough of exploits that are beyond our comprehension. Here you may see how noteworthy were those of his vassals too.

'Look at this man with the eyes flashing anger as he bids his defeated and petulant ward collect his scattered forces and return to challenge the victor on the field. The youth goes back, accompanied by his elder, and thanks to him snatches victory from defeat. Egas Moniz is the old warrior's name, a shining exemplar to all true lieges.

'In this other picture you see him, stripped of his fine silken garments and with a halter about his neck, about to deliver himself and his children into the enemy's hands because of the young king's refusal to own allegiance to the

Castilian, as Moniz had undertaken he would. By dint of prudence and assurances he had secured the raising of a siege the end of which was only too clear, and now, in order that his sovereign may go free, he condemns himself and his wife and family to suffering.

'The Consul Postumius Albinus did not do as much when, having carelessly invited defeat at the Caudine Forks, he was compelled by the Samnites to pass under the victor's yoke. He, repudiated by his fellow-Romans, staunchly gave himself up alone to the enemy. Egas Moniz sacrificed his blameless wife and children too, a much more grievous expiation.

'Look now at this warrior emerging from ambush and falling upon the king who had invested his stronghold. In no time the king is in his hands and the siege lifted, an exploit worthy of Mars himself. Here you see him again, this time on board ship, dealing death to the Moslems at sea as previously on land and carrying off, with their galleys, the glory of Portugal's first naval victory. He is Fuas Roupinho, a man equally famous in both elements. Later he will set fire to a Moslem fleet under the very heights of Ceuta. And note how, in such a just and holy war, he is well content to die in battle, his happy soul eluding the enemy as it soars triumphantly to Heaven, bearing the palm of the righteous.

'This picture shows a contingent of foreigners, as you may see by their dress, landing from a powerful fleet to help Afonso I in his assault on Lisbon, in which they bore themselves like true crusaders. See here the famous knight Heinrich and the miracle-working palm-tree which sprang up close by his tomb, in divine recognition of the devotion of these German martyrs of Christ.

'Here is a priest brandishing his sword against Arronches,

which he captures in revenge for Leiria, that had earlier fallen into Moslem hands: he is the Prior Teotónio. But look now at Santarem under siege, and note the confidence with which the first man to scale the walls raises the standard of the five shields. Here he is again with Sancho I, waging fierce and triumphant battle against the Moslems in Andalusia, disrupting the enemy ranks, slaying their standard-bearer and trampling under foot the pennant of Seville. Mem Moniz is his name, a living portrait of the same valour that his father Egas bore with him to the grave, and worthily to be remembered in connection with both banners, his country's that he exalted and the enemy's that he abased.

'Look at this knight climbing down from the watch-tower by the aid of his lance, with the heads of the two men who were on guard as trophy, and returning to the ambush where he had left his followers. See how, by a combination of subterfuge and daring, he gains possession of Evora. It was in memory of this unparalleled feat that the city afterwards adopted as its coat-of-arms the figure of the stalwart Giraldo the Fearless, with the two heads in his hand.

'Here you may see a Castilian who fell out with his king, Alfonso IX, over an ancient family feud with the house of Lara and threw in his lot with the Moslem, so proclaiming himself the enemy of the Portuguese as well. But when with a force of the infidels he then occupied Abrantes, observe how a Portuguese, Martim Lopes, with a very scanty band launched a daring counter-attack, defeated him and took him prisoner, thus despoiling him of his victor's wreath of palm and laurel.

'And here comes another fighting churchman, exchanging his golden crozier for a lance of steel. See how resolute he is in the midst of doubters over joining issue with the daring Moslem. And look at the sign from Heaven that is vouchsafed him and that enables him to infuse new spirit into his small troop. Note how, within a short space of time, the kings of Cordoba and Seville and those of Badajoz and Jaen as well are routed, and more than routed, killed, a veritable miracle from God, surpassing the power of man. Now it is the turn of Alcácer to be humbled, in spite of its defences and its wall of steel, before this same Bishop Mateus of Lisbon who is there crowned with glory.

'This next is a proud Master of Santiago, Portuguese by birth, who has come back from Castile to join in the conquest of the Algarve and can find no place there capable of withstanding him. With skill, valour and fortune all on his side, towns and castles fall to him in open assault. Tavira was one of his conquests, in revenge for the seven Portuguese who, while out hunting in time of truce, were there set upon and slain. Silves was another, won by astute tactics from an enemy who had earlier needed a mighty army to occupy it. Paio Correia was his name, a man envied by all for his skill and bravery.

'And do not miss these three knights-errant who by their prowess in challenges, jousts, and tourneys, in which they carried off many a public trophy, left a lasting name behind them in France and Spain. You see them here arriving as adventurers in Castile, where, to the hurt of some among their competitors, all the prizes in martial contests were theirs. These bodies are those of the haughty knights who challenged the leader of the three, Gonçalo Ribeira, a name that need not fear oblivion.

'Next comes one whom Fame has carried so far that none of all his predecessors can now content her. When his country's fate hung on a slender thread, he sustained it on his own broad shoulders. Observe how, flushed with anger, he chides the people for their unworthy lack of confidence and the lethargy that would let them accept an alien yoke, and makes them opt instead for the congenial sway of a king of their own.

'Note how, guided by God and his sacred destiny, and invoking all his prudence and daring, he achieves the seeming impossible by overthrowing single-handed the might of Castile. And see here the renewed havoc he has wrought in a second encounter with that fierce and populous nation that dwells between the Guadalquivir and the Guadiana. Consider what a magnificent and sweeping victory is once again the reward of such skill, dash, and bravery.

'But look: the Portuguese forces, lacking the presence of their devout leader, are on the verge of defeat. He has withdrawn to invoke the Blessed Trinity in prayer. See how impetuously they seek him out, telling him that there is no withstanding such overwhelming pressure and beseeching him to come and give new courage to the waverers. And note with what saintly assurance he replies that the moment is not yet, speaking as one who has complete trust in God that he will shortly give him the victory. So Numa Pompilius, on being told that his enemies were overrunning the country, made answer to the bearer of such grim tidings: "And I am making sacrifice to the gods."

'Should you be curious to know the name of this God-fearing man who dared so much and so valiantly, it is Nuno Alvares. Portuguese Scipio, he might well be called; but the other is a prouder name still. Happy the country that bore such a son! Or rather sire: for as long as the sun shall encircle this globe that Ceres and Neptune divide between them, so long shall it mourn the loss of such a patriot.

'Here you may see the booty won by another captain of

but a handful of men in this same war, when he vanquished the Commanders of two Military Orders and recovered the ill-gotten spoils they were boldly carrying off. This other incident shows his lance again running with Castilian blood when, impelled by ardent affection, he set out to rescue a bosom friend whose loyalty had caused him to be taken prisoner. He is Pero Rodrigues do Landroal.

'This scene depicts a traitor and the price he paid for his perjury and foul deceit. Gil Fernandes of Elvas is the man who brought him to book and made him pay the supreme penalty, afterwards laying waste the country around Jerez until it ran with the blood of its Castilian masters. And look: here is the Admiral Rui Pereira, confronting the enemy's galleys and shielding his own with the sheer determination of his countenance.

'See now the seventeen Portuguese on this hillock, with what bravery they resist four hundred Castilians who have hemmed them in on all sides and are trying to make them surrender. The assailants will discover to their cost that the Portuguese are not merely on the defensive, but are capable of attack as well. This was a stand deserving of immortality; noteworthy in olden times, it remains no less so in ours.

'In the days when Viriato so ennobled himself with his great deeds of daring, history tells how three hundred of our countrymen once fought against a thousand Romans, giving them a memorable beating and bequeathing to us the injunction never to be afraid of superior numbers; and since then we have shown a thousand times that we are not.

'Look at these two princes, Pedro and Henrique, noble offspring of João I. Pedro won for himself a fame in Germany that death cannot efface. Henrique achieved renown as a great ocean discoverer. He was also the first to enter the gates of Ceuta, so pricking the swollen bubble of Moslem vanity.

'This other is Count Pedro de Meneses, who as Governor of Ceuta withstood two sieges against all the might of Barbary. And you can see here his son, Duarte de Meneses, in might and daring a very Mars on earth. Not content with defending Alcácer-Seguer against the enemy hordes, he defended too the precious life of his king, using his own as a shield, and losing it.

'And there is many another figure you might have seen here, whom the artists would certainly have painted had they had the brushes and the colours: I mean the honours, the rewards, the favours on which the arts are nourished. It is the fault of their degenerate successors that they are not: for degeneracy, beyond a doubt, there has been, and a withdrawing from the lustre and the valour of their forerunners, in a generation so depraved in its pleasures and vanities.

'Those distinguished ancestors who founded great families did great things in the cause of virtue and to the end of starting a noble line. How blind they were! For if, by their labours, they spread afar their own name and reputation, they invariably consigned their descendants to oblivion by bequeathing to them a life of slothfulness, that is enough to undermine all high resolve.

'Others there are who have achieved rank and possessions without coming of illustrious stock. The fault here lies with monarchs who will sometimes shower on a favourite rewards a thousandfold more generous than are forthcoming for wisdom and valour. And such men prefer not to see their ancestors depicted on canvas, fearing lest the result prove unflattering. As for seeing them portrayed in verse,

verse might be their natural enemy, so profoundly do they dislike it.

'I admit that, all this notwithstanding, some descendants of noble families and rich houses may be found who worthily maintain the great name they have inherited, pursuing a way of life that is at once distinguished and beyond reproach. And if the torch of their forbears does not burn any more brightly in their hands, at least it has not gone out nor grown dim. But the artist rarely comes across examples of these.'

So Paulo da Gama expounded the notable deeds that the painter's skill had there depicted with such convincing realism. The Catual's eyes had never wandered from the heroic record; asking a thousand questions, he had listened with intense pleasure to the explanation of all the battles there presented to his gaze. When, accompanied by the Naires, he at length took his leave of the great vessel in search of the repose that gentle night affords the weary frame, the great luminary was already sinking beneath the horizon, carrying its rays to the antipodes, and the light of day was fading.

Meanwhile the soothsayers who by their diabolical art read the future in the entrails of sacrificial victims, and whose prestige is always high in the absence of true religion, were by the king's instructions studiously invoking their lore to divine the significance of the coming of these foreigners from the unknown lands of Iberia. And now the devil, speaking true for once, revealed to one of them how the newcomers would mean their perpetual subjection to an alien yoke and the destruction of their lives and property. The augur was astounded, and hastened in alarm to tell the king his interpretation of the fearsome signs that his inspection of the entrails had brought to light.

Next it was the turn of the odious Bacchus, whose hatred still showed no signs of abating. Assuming the guise of the notorious false prophet of the line of Ishmael, he appeared in a dream to a devout Mohammedan priest who shared his animosity against the one true and supreme religion, and spoke to him thus: 'Be on your guard, my people, while there is still time, against the evil designs of this enemy from across the seas.' At this the Moslem awoke with a terrified start; but, thinking it was but an ordinary dream, he went peacefully to sleep again, his mind at ease.

Bacchus appeared to him a second time, saying: 'Do you not recognize me, the great lawgiver Mahomet, who revealed to your forefathers the faith in which you have been brought up, and without which many of you would have been baptized? You sluggard: here I watch over you, and you fall asleep! One day you will realize that these strangers mean a very real threat to the faith I gave to mankind in its ignorance. So far they are few in number and weak: see to it that they are resisted in every way. When the sun first rises it is easy to look straight at it; but once it is high in the heavens a steady gaze means blindness. That same blindness will be yours if you do not nip this danger in the bud.'

He vanished, and the dream ended. The priest leapt from his bed, shaking with terror as the poison worked in his veins, and called to his servants for a light. Then, as soon as dawn had shown its serene, angelic face, he called together the leaders of his accursed sect and told them the story of his vision. Conflicting opinions were voiced as they severally weighed the situation. Deeds of treachery, perfidy and deceit were subtly cogitated and worked out. In the end, however, rash counsels were discarded in favour of a more astute and cunning plan, which was to win over the king's advisers with bribes and work the destruction of the Portuguese through them.

And so, suborning them privily with gold and other gifts, they got the leaders of the land on their side, persuading them with much plausible argument that the newcomers were a restless breed who lived a life of piracy and rapine on the western seas, owning no king and respecting no laws, whether of men or of God, and such as must prove the ruin of India.

What a heavy charge it is on the monarch who would govern well to see that his counsellors and intimates are men of conscience and integrity, genuinely devoted to his interests! His own position being the most exalted of all, he can ill inform himself of affairs that do not happen to fall under his own eye other than by the reports of his ministers. Yet neither would I have him accept without further question the clear and forthright conscience that is to be found beneath the humble cloak of the poor, where ambition too may possibly lie concealed. When, moreover, a man is good and just and saintly in all things, he will have little judgement in worldly matters; for the tranquil innocence which fixes its gaze on God alone is in no position to keep abreast of them.

But the self-seeking Catuals who ruled this heathen people allowed themselves to be persuaded by the infernal priests, and deferred a decision on the Portuguese request.

Da Gama's only concern in their deliberations was that he should not be prevented from carrying back to his king a trustworthy account of the world he had discovered; and to this end he bent his activities, knowing well that King Manoel, on receipt of his information, would send ships, men and arms sufficient to reduce to his sway and to the Christian faith the whole vast expanse of land and sea. For himself, he was but a diligent explorer of the territories of the East.

He accordingly resolved to have further word with the Samorin himself, obtain his answer, and be off, for he had already sensed the opposition that these ill-disposed individuals were creating to everything he sought to do.

But it was scarcely to be wondered at that the king, so credulous in the matter of divinations, and especially now with the confirming of these by the Moslems, should have been alarmed by the base and lying report. His ignoble heart was in the grip of chill fear. His grasping nature, on the other hand, pulled him in the opposite direction, cupidity inflaming in him a desire that would not be quenched; for he saw clearly the very great advantage there would be to him in concluding, on a basis of sincerity and justice, the long-term treaty offered by the king of Portugal. In his consultations, however, he found this point of view strongly combated, for bribery was producing its effect on his ministers.

At length he sent for da Gama and said to him: 'If you will confess to me the plain, unvarnished truth, I will pardon you your crime. I have reliable information that the embassy you gave me from your king was false, for you have no king, nor native land, to command your love. You live the life of a vagabond. What king or lord of farthest Hesperia would be so unbridled in his folly as to dispatch ships and fleets on voyages so hazardous and so remote?

'And supposing your king does hold sway over great and powerful territories, what rich presents do you bring me from him in token of the truth of these unknown things you tell of? Friendship between rulers of high estate is cemented by exquisite fabrics and the like magnificent presents. The mere word of a roving mariner is not enough.

'Perchance you have been exiled. If so, and provided you were men of rank in your own country, you will be hospitably received in my kingdom, for to the brave all the world is their homeland. If you are pirates, hardened to the sea, you may say so without fear of infamy or death; since man must live, and there has never yet been an age when the urge was not all-powerful.'

Da Gama heard him to the end. He had had his inklings of the insidious wiles that the Moslems in their hatred were weaving against him, and that explained the king's so unjustifiable insinuations. With the lofty confidence the occasion demanded and a tone that imposed full credence – it was the Venus of the Acidalian fountain who inspired it – he now spoke these words of wisdom:

'Were it not, great King, that the crimes our first fathers committed in their malice provoked that vessel of iniquity, Mahomet, to show himself such a cruel scourge to Christendom, sowing perpetual hatred among the children of Adam with his false and shameful creed, you could never have conceived such evil suspicions. No great good, it is true, is ever achieved save after great adversity, and in every enterprise fear treads hard on the heels of hope, which springs from a heart keyed up with apprehension. And so you show so little confidence in this true story of mine, paying no heed to the reasons you would easily find on the other side had you not put your trust in those who do not deserve it.

'If I lived by plunder alone, a wanderer on the face of the ocean or an exile from my native land, what, think you, would have driven me so far in search of a remote and unknown haven? What hopes or what self-interest would have sustained me as I weathered the tempestuous seas, the Antarctic cold, the heat of the torrid zone? If you ask me for presents rich and rare as warranty of the truth of what I speak, know that I come merely as an explorer out to discover these strange climes wherein Nature has set your ancient kingdom. Should fortune so smile on me, however, as to return me to my native land, then you shall see with how sumptuous a gift I shall make known to you my safe arrival.

'And if it seem to you unthinkable that a king of farthest Hesperia should send me to you, consider that to the sublime heart that beats in a royal breast nothing that is feasible is deemed great. So greatly daring, so exalted is the temper of the Portuguese, it clearly demands an ampler measure of belief, a loftier faith such as can credit it with fortitude of this calibre.

'I would have you know that it is now many years since earlier kings of ours, determined not to be beaten by the toils and perils that attend great enterprises, first launched voyages of discovery across the restless ocean in the resolve to ascertain its farthest boundaries and the whereabouts of the most distant shores it lapped. It was an undertaking worthy of Henrique [the Navigator], that noble scion of the fortunate João I, the pioneer who crossed the sea to occupy Ceuta, ejecting its last inhabitant from the home of his fathers.

'Applying his skill and rare ingenuity to the building of ships, Henrique succeeded in discovering the regions of the southern hemisphere where the constellations Argo, Hydra, Lepus, and Ara shine in the heavens. Then, waxing bolder with the success of his first expeditions, his men gradually ventured farther and farther into the unknown, and we who came after have picked up the torch and continued.

Leaving far behind us those who dwell in the burning tropics, we have seen the southernmost peoples of Africa, in whose sky the Great Bear is never visible.

'And so, with firmness of heart and resolve, we have vanquished fickle fortune until now we have come to set up our last landmark in this distant abode of yours. Conquering the mighty ocean with its sudden fearsome tempests, we have sailed even to here, and all we would ask of you is a token that we may carry back to our own sovereign.

'This, O King, is the truth; nor would I spin so long a preamble, nor one so fanciful and so pointless, for a reward as slender and uncertain as would be mine were it not as I have stated. I should have preferred to seek repose on the cruel, heaving bosom of the deep, living the life of a wicked pirate and amassing wealth from the labours of others.

'If Your Majesty is prepared to accept this true story of mine for what it is, sincere and aboveboard, then grant me your answer and grant it speedily, that I may taste the pleasure of returning home. Should I still seem to you to be speaking falsely, consider the extent to which reason is on my side, as will be obvious to any clear judgement. The truth of the matter may readily be perceived.'

The king observed the assurance with which da Gama argued his assertions and conceived a complete confidence in him, being now fully persuaded that he had lied in nothing. Pondering on the sufficiency of his protestations, he found them backed with all the weight of valid authority, and decided that the Catuals were under a misapprehension; though he judged them wrongly in this, for they were merely corrupt.

He was the more disposed to respect da Gama and accept his word, rather than that of the lying Moslems, by the thought of the gain he looked for from the alliance with Portugal. And so he now bade him return to the ships forthwith, assuring him that no hurt would be done him and that he might send ashore any goods he had for sale or for barter against spices. He inquired particularly about wares that were not to be had in India, should da Gama have brought any such from that far country where the land portion of the globe gave way to ocean.

The Captain took his leave of the royal presence and, rejoining the Catual who was in charge of him, asked him for a boat to take him out to the fleet, his own being off-shore. But the wicked Governor, who was busy contriving new pitfalls for the Portuguese, replied only with delays and difficulties, evading his request. He set out with him for the wharf, but this was merely to get him as far as possible from the palace and be able to vent whatever malice might suggest without the king's knowledge.

There, at a safe distance, he made him promises that a boat would be forthcoming, but suggested that he put off his departure until the following day. Da Gama had been slow to realize it, but with all this procrastination it was now clear to him that the other was definitely in league with the Moslems in their abominable plot.

For this Catual, the chief of those who governed the cities of the great Samorin, was one of the number they had bought over, and it was on him principally that they relied for the success of their plans. He was therefore actively in the conspiracy, and had no intention of failing them. Da Gama pressed his request to be taken out to the ships, reminding him that this was the Samorin's command, but to no effect. What was the reason, he then asked, for keeping him from bringing his Portuguese wares ashore? No one had the right to countermand a royal order.

The mercenary Catual paid scant heed to such protests. Instead, casting about in his mind for some really subtle way of achieving his diabolical end, he found himself plotting, now how he might run the hated enemy through with his sword, now how to set fire to the ships and prevent the Portuguese to the last man from ever seeing their native land again. For this was the sole aim of the Moslems in their infernal counsels, to see to it that not one of them ever got back home, so that the king of Portugal should never know where these eastern lands lay.

And hence, in the upshot, da Gama was unable to take off, the heathen Catual refusing him permission. Nor could he go without permission, for the other had caused every canoe there was to be put out of reach. Da Gama still argued and expostulated, but the Catual's only reply was to tell him to bid his vessels draw nearer inshore and so lessen the coming and going. To have the fleet lie so far off, he said, betokened a hostile and dishonest intent. It was the mark of sincerity and loyalty to fear no peril from one's friends.

From these words da Gama discreetly inferred that the Catual wished to have the ships nearer to hand the better to fall upon them with fire and sword once the time came for the dropping of pretences. He fell to thinking by what means he might most effectively counter all the wickedness that was being devised against him; apprehending every contingency, he sought to prepare to meet them all.

Everyone knows how a mirror of burnished steel or polished glass will catch the sun's rays and reflect them in another direction, and we have all seen how a youngster, picking one up with idle hands, will play the beam so that it flickers tremulously now on this part of the house, now on that, now on the walls, now on the roof. In the same way the captive da Gama's thoughts were darting now here, now there, when suddenly he remembered the possibility that Coelho might already be waiting for him on the beach with his own ship's boats, as he had ordered. He managed to dispatch a messenger secretly, bidding him, if he were there, return to the fleet and be on his guard against the traps he had cause to fear the Moslems were laying for them.

Such must the captain be who would not only follow in the footsteps of the great but be their peer: flying in imagination to every part of the field, foreseeing dangers and averting them by all the arts and subtleties of war, reading the enemy's thoughts and taking him in by his ruses, being prepared, in short, for everything. The leader who says 'I never thought of that' shall never be praised by me.

The Catual meantime continued adamant in his refusal to release da Gama unless he first ordered the fleet to come inshore. But the Captain was no less firm in his resolve and, fired now with a noble anger, he set these threats at naught. Rather than hazard the present safety of his sovereign's ships, he preferred that all the weight of any villainy the enemy's malice and daring might hatch should fall on him alone.

All that night he was detained, and part of the following day. He then determined to go back to the Samorin, but this his now numerous guard would not permit either.

The heathen then made him a new proposal, fearing the pains and penalties that would be his should the king come to know of his malicious behaviour, as he soon would if da Gama were to be held there any longer. This was that da Gama should send instructions for all the saleable merchandise he had to be brought on shore, where it might be bartered or sold at leisure. He who refused to trade, he said, could only be intending war.

Da Gama saw through the evil intentions his wicked heart concealed. He consented none the less, calculating that with the goods he could buy his way to freedom, but stipulated that the other should provide suitable craft for the purpose, for he was not prepared to risk his own boats anywhere where they might be seized or detained by the enemy. The canoes put out accordingly to fetch the merchandise, and da Gama sent a note to his brother asking him to include articles with which he might purchase his ransom.

The goods were duly brought ashore, under the supervision of the infamous Catual. Alvaro de Braga and Diogo Dias were put in charge of them, with orders to sell them for what they might fetch. And now, for those with eyes to see, the Catual provided an eloquent demonstration of how much stronger in the mercenary heart is the pull of gain than of obligation, command or entreaty, for in return for some of the wares he at last agreed to release his captive. This he did on the reckoning that the goods were sufficient guarantee of a greater return than he could look for by continuing to hold him.

To the Captain, once on board ship, it was plain that any thought of going back on shore, with the risk of being held a second time, was not in his interest, and he was content to stay there and rest. So there he stayed, biding his time until he could see what the future held in store. In the basely corrupt and avaricious Catual he no longer placed any trust.

And here the curious and judicious reader may consider how potent, in rich and poor alike, is depraved self-interest, that fatal thirst for gain whose compulsion knows no bounds. Polymnestor, king of Thrace, slew Polydorus merely to get possession of his treasure. Jupiter, in the guise of a shower of gold, penetrated the redoubtable stronghold where Acrisius had immured his daughter Danae. Swayed by avarice, Tarpeia delivered to the Sabines the citadel on the Capitoline Hill in return for their bracelets of gleaming gold, only to perish of suffocation under the weight of them.

Gold will reduce the strongest fortress, it will turn friends into traitors and deceivers, constrain the noble to acts of infamy, make men betray their leaders to the foe. It can corrupt a maiden's purity, so that she no longer fears to endanger fame and honour, and will debase on occasion the very pursuit of learning, blinding men's judgement and their consciences. Gold causes authorities to be interpreted with something more than subtlety, makes and unmakes laws, turns ordinary men into perjurers, and kings, times without number, into tyrants. Even among those who are wholly dedicated to the service of God Omnipotent you will find countless examples where this enchanter has corrupted and misled, under cover, withal, of virtue.

CANTO

9

THE two factors had their wares on offer in the city for a long time without making any sales, for the infidels through their lying wiles kept the local traders from purchasing. Their whole purpose and intention now was to delay the discoverers until the arrival of ships from Mecca, counting on these to destroy them.

Far away in the Red Sea, where Ptolemy of Egypt once founded the city called, after his sister, Arsinoe (its name now is Suez), lies that other famous city of Mecca, whose greatness had its origin in the idle and profane superstition of Mahomet's holy well. Jidda, its nearby port, is the most prosperous commercial centre in the whole of the Red Sea, and a source of rich and very acceptable profit to the Sultan of Egypt. And from Jidda there sailed each year for Malabar, across the Indian Ocean, an impressive fleet of large vessels in search of spices, under agreement between the countries.

It was the Moslems' hope that these vessels, by reason of their size and strength, would join issue with the interlopers who were seeking to steal their trade, and burn them out; and so confident were they of help from this quarter that they no longer wanted anything more of the Portuguese than that they should tarry long enough for those from Mecca to arrive.

But he who rules Heaven and earth provides, well in advance, the means appropriate to his every end. Monsaide was his chosen instrument for the warning of da Gama – he was to merit Paradise thereby – and in him he now implanted sentiments of affectionate concern.

Far from being on their guard with one of their own religion, the Moslems had made Monsaide privy to all their machinations. He had been a frequent visitor to the ships as they lay off-shore, and had pondered with distress on the unjustifiable wrong that the evil Saracens had in store for them.

And now he told the wary da Gama not merely of the baseness and cruelty they were harbouring in their minds, but about the yearly fleet from Mecca in Arabia and of the eagerness with which his co-religionists awaited its arrival as an instrument to the undoing of the Portuguese. He added that the Arabs came heavily manned and gunned, and that in the indifferent state of the Captain's defences he might well come off second-best.

Da Gama had already been studying the weather, which was now favourable to his departure; and, having given up hope of any more encouraging reply from the Samorin, whose good graces the Moslems so obviously monopolized, he sent a message to the two factors bidding them return on board with all possible secrecy, for he did not want to raise fresh difficulties from the noising abroad of this sudden summons.

It was not long, however, before rumour, this time well enough founded, did take wing. For the factors were seen leaving the city, and were detained. When the news reached da Gama he acted at once, seizing as hostages some Indians who had gone out to the ships to sell precious stones. These happened to be wealthy merchants long established in Calicut and well known among the upper classes there.

Their failure to return was accordingly noticed, and it was inferred that da Gama was holding them.

The crews were working now with a will, each at his post. Here they were busy at the capstan, applying their chests to the bars as if they would break them, while others tugged at the anchor-rope; there men were hanging from the yardarm unfurling the sail until, with a mighty noise, it shook itself free.

It was just then that, with an uproar louder still, the news broke on the king that the fleet was weighing anchor with all speed; for the wives and children of the hostages had hastened to the Samorin's presence and, beside themselves with grief, were lamenting clamorously the loss of husbands and fathers.

The Samorin brushed aside the opposition of the Moslems and ordered the two Portuguese to be set free immediately with all their property, that he might get his own people back again. With them he sent apologies for the double-dealing. Da Gama received the prisoners with a better grace than he did the excuses and, returning some of the natives, he set sail and was off.

As he followed the coast to the south, he reflected on the failure of his efforts to obtain from the pagan ruler a treaty of peace as firm foundation for the trade he aimed at. But at least he was leaving behind, in this great country of the East, a land that was no longer unknown, and now he was on his way back to his own beloved country, bearing with him, not the news of the discovery alone, but eloquent proofs.

For in addition to the natives he had seized forcibly from among those sent by the Samorin to deliver back the factors, he had obtained by purchase pepper, mace from the Banda Islands, the nutmegs and cloves that were the pride of the new-found Moluccas, and finally cinnamon, the key to the wealth, fame, and beauty of Ceylon.

That he had so much was due to the diligence of the faithful Monsaide, whom he had also brought away with him; for the Moor, under divine inspiration, was desirous of becoming a Christian. Happy Moor, thus rescued by God's clemency from the darkness of error and shown, when so far from home and country, the way to his true abode!

And now the fortunate vessels had left the steaming coast astern and set their prows once more for that southern outpost of Nature, the Cape of Good Hope. Once more, timorous-glad, they faced the grim terrors of the uncertain ocean. But this time they were Lisbon-bound, with joyous tidings and news of the East; and there was not a man among them who did not dwell, as on a joy so perfect that his heart could ill contain it, on the pleasure of seeing once again his beloved Portugal and his so cherished home and dear ones, of recounting his rare peregrinations across the seas and the divers climes and peoples he had seen, and of achieving at last the merited reward for all his far-flung trials and tribulations.

It was many a long year since Venus, appointed by Jupiter to be the good genius of the Portuguese, had first bestowed on them her special favour and guidance. Just now, anxious to gladden the dreary monotony of the voyage, she was busy devising some compensation for all the perils so manfully endured, some crowning tribute to their so arduous achievement. Recapitulating in her mind the vast expanse of ocean over which they had sailed and all the toils that Bacchus had strewn in their path, she resolved on a project she had long been toying with in fancy as fitting requital.

This was to find them some haven of leisure and delight in that watery domain, some retreat where her mariners might refresh their weary humanity, a respite from the labours that consume man's brief existence. Sensibly she decided to inform her son Cupid, since it was through him she had it in her power to bring gods down to earth and to raise mere mortals to the skies.

Having thought it all over, she decided to prepare for them, there in mid-ocean, a magic island beauteous with flowers and verdure, one of many she had dotted over the open seas in addition to those in the Mediterranean that owned her sovereign sway. There she would have the loveliest of the ocean nymphs await the brave fellows, to enchant their eyes and vanquish their hearts with their singing and dancing; for she was proposing to work secretly on the nymphs' affections and predispose each to a readier will to please whichever of the Portuguese should catch her fancy. It was the same stratagem she had once invoked to secure for Aeneas, her own son by Anchises, a friendly reception in Carthage, the scene of Dido's subtle bargain over the amount of land an ox-hide might enclose.

And so she went in search of Cupid, without whose aid she was powerless in these matters. He had helped her in that other enterprise of old, and now he would help her again. Harnessing the doves and swans to her chariot, she set out, the air filled with the lascivious kisses her gentle steeds kept throwing to one another. Where her course lay the wind was calmed, and only the graceful motion of her passage disturbed the air.

Soon she was over the hills of Cyprus, where her archer son was then engaged in marshalling a force of lesser Cupids for a major expedition against rebellious mankind, that had lately lapsed into serious error through giving its heart to things meant to be used, not to be loved.

There was Actaeon, so austere in his devotion to the chase, so obsessed by its irrational, brutish pleasures that he eschewed the company of his kind, and especially of lovely womankind, in order to pursue ugly, savage beasts. His punishment was bitter-sweet, for he was to be given a glimpse of Diana in all her beauty – and let him beware that he be not finally devoured by his own dogs, that he also loves.

There were rulers all over the world among whom not one was to be found concerned only with the public good, for their love was fixed wholly on themselves and on others equally self-centred. There were those who frequented the courts of kings selling as sound doctrine what was but adulation, which ill permits the stripling plant to grow up strong and free from weeds.

As for those whose duty it was to dispense to the poor the love of God and to treat all men charitably, they were in love only with power and riches, and made an empty show of justice and integrity. Right to them meant ugly tyranny, harshness, severity to no purpose. They made laws in favour of the king and allowed such as favoured the people to lapse.

Cupid observed, in short, that no one loved what he ought to be loving but only the objects of unworthy desire, and he was not prepared to see just and rigorous punishment deferred any longer.

And so he was assembling his levies, determined to have adequate backing in the fray he looked for with these misguided people who refused him their obedience. Many of his winged minions were already busy about their various preparations, some sharpening darts, others shaping arrow-shafts; and as they worked they sang songs of love and its ways, a sweet, concerted chorus in which, if the words were pleasing, the melody was divine.

The forges where they struck the piercing arrow-heads were fired with burning hearts as fuel, that still palpitated with life. For water to temper the metal they used the tears of wretched lovers. The ever-living flame was desire, that burns but does not consume. Some were even now trying their hand on the stony hearts of rude plebeians, and the air resounded with the repeated sighings of the wounded whenever an arrow found its mark.

The healing of the wounds was the care of beautiful nymphs, whose succour not merely restored life where it was endangered but gave life to others as yet unborn. Yet if some of the nymphs were fair, others were ugly, according to the nature of the wound; for when poison is coursing through the veins its cure demands at times a bitter antidote. And among the victims some lay bound in chains, the result of the incantations of crafty spell-binders: this can happen when the arrow is tipped with secret herbs.

With these inexpert youths thus loosing their shafts at random, there resulted a thousand ill-concerted infatuations among their pitiable victims. Even among heroes of high estate examples abound of unworthy and even criminal passion, as witness the maidens Byblis and Myrrha, the Assyrian Ninyas or Amnon of Judaea. How often has the prince's heart been smitten with love of a shepherdess! How often have great ladies been taken, as Venus herself was once in Vulcan's net, with common and uncouth lovers! Some men are for ever awaiting the hours of darkness, others ever scaling walls and roofs. For myself, I blame Venus rather than Cupid for all such culpable aberrations.

But now the swans were bringing the dainty chariot gently to rest on the green sward, and Venus, her cheeks like roses framed in snow, was quick to alight. Cupid greeted her joyously, and all his minions hastened to kiss the hand of the goddess of love.

She wasted no time. Throwing her arms around her son, she addressed him confidently. 'My dear boy,' she said, 'on whom, now as always, all my powers depend, you were ever fearless, even against the bolts of Jupiter, and I want your help now for a very special purpose.

'You know that I have long had a particular care for the Portuguese – my friends the Fates told me of their worship and esteem for me – and you are well aware of all they have been going through of late. Seeing that they are following so closely in the footsteps of my Romans of old, I want to give them all the help I can – all we both can.

'In India they were much molested by the wiles of hateful Bacchus, and on the heaving ocean they have suffered such buffetings as might well have not merely exhausted, but finished them. On that same ocean, that they have always found a source of dread, I want them now to find repose and to enjoy some measure of reward and glory for their immortal labours.

'My idea, now that they are on their way home after discovering a new world, is that the Nereids down in their watery depths should be smitten and inflamed with love for them, and should come up and await them on an island I am getting ready in the midst of the waves, which I am bedecking with all the gifts that Flora and Zephyr between them can bestow.

'There, amidst an endless plenty of food and drink laid out in gleaming crystal halls, the wines perfumed and the goblets draped with roses, with inviting couches and the Nereids more inviting still, replete, in short, with a thousand delicate delights, there I would have the loving, love-struck nymphs attend these mariners, in a mood to make them free of all their eyes may covet. I was born in Neptune's domains, and I want to see them peopled with a breed that will combine strength and beauty.

'As for the base and wicked world that dares to challenge your sway, let it take note and learn that neither adamantine walls nor gloomy hypocrisy can avail against it. If your undying flame burn even on the waters, who is there on land can believe himself immune?'

So Venus proposed, and her wayward son prepared at once to obey. He called for his bow of precious ivory and tipped his arrows with gold. Venus made room for him in her chariot, a note of wanton satisfaction in her gesture, then, loosening rein, gave the swans their head.

Cupid remarked that he would need the services of a certain notorious go-between, one who had worked against him, it was true, many a time, but who often again had helped him in his designs. This was Fame, the bold and boastful giant-goddess, the speaker both of falsehood and of truth, with a hundred eyes to see and a thousand mouths to broadcast, in her rovings, all she saw.

They went to find her, and sent her on ahead to sing with trumpet-notes the seafarers' praises, charging her to pitch these higher than those of any she had ever praised before. This she did, and her report rippled its way to the caverns of the deep and there spread far and wide. What the goddess spoke this time was true, and was accepted as true, for she had taken Credulity along with her.

Such rare praises, the tidings of such outstanding qualities, had their effect on the hearts even of the gods whom Bacchus had inflamed against the heroes, and inclined them somewhat in their favour. The feminine heart, that more lightly abandons its earlier decisions, was already prepared to count it misplaced zeal and cruelty that had led them to wish such bravery ill.

With this, Cupid let fly his arrows one by one, until the sea groaned under the impact. Some went straight through the restless waves, others described a more circuitous course. All found their mark, and the nymphs began to utter most ardent sighs, that welled from the secret depths of their being. Each one was smitten, though none had yet seen the face of him she loved; for the ear in these matters is as vulnerable as the eye.

The indomitable youth then drew bow once again, more vigorously this time than ever, for on Tethys, who was ever the most hostile to the Portuguese, he wanted to inflict the deepest wound of all.

And now his quiver was empty, nor was there left in all the ocean a nymph alive. Wounded, indeed, they still drew breath, but only to the extent of realizing that the wound was fatal.

But let the surging billows make way, for look, Venus has seen to the remedy: riding the blue sea, the bellying white sails come into view. Now ardent love can make reciprocal answer to the passion that fires the maiden hearts, provided, that is, that native modesty show a due deference to Venus's every behest.

Led by Venus herself, the whole beauteous company of the Nereids had already set out for the island, engaging as they went in the choral dances that were their custom. Once there, the lovely goddess told them of her own behaviour on the innumerable occasions when she fell in love; and they, now completely in thrall to the gentle emotion, hung on her every word.

The fleet continued to forge its way across the mighty deep, the beloved homeland ever its goal. It was on the look-out now for a spot where it could take in fresh water for the long voyage still ahead, when with sudden joy, just as dawn was breaking gently overhead, the ships all spotted together the Isle of Love.

They were still far off when they saw it in all its freshness and beauty. Venus was wafting it over the waves towards them, as a white sail is wafted by the breeze, to ensure that they should not pass by without making harbour, this being her design and she being, after all, all-powerful. As soon as she saw that the sailors had spied it and were heading that way, she made it fast and firm, as did Jupiter once with Delos, that Latona might there give birth in safety to Apollo and Diana the huntress.

The prows were cleaving the sea towards a tranquil, curving bay with its glistening strand that Venus had dotted with rosy shells. From the island, all joy and charm and loveliness, there rose three comely hills, their noble grace adorned with luxuriant vegetation. Limpid streams flowed from their summits, murmuring as they rippled over white pebbly beds: hence the lushness of the verdure.

A pleasant valley set between the hills caught the pellucid waters, forming a lake that was breath-taking in its beauty; and overhanging its edge was a graceful cluster of trees, preparing its toilet, one might have said, as it studied its reflection in the gleaming pool that mirrored every detail.

But there was no counting the trees as they soared skywards, all laden with fragrant, luscious fruit. There were orange-trees, their crop the colour of Daphne's golden tresses, citron-trees weighted until they seemed to be leaning on the ground for support for their yellow burden, while the air was redolent with the odour of delicately moulded lemons, like a maiden's breasts.

Ennobling the heights with their leafy crowns were poplars, the tree sacred to Hercules, Apollo's favourite laurels, the myrtles of Venus, and Cybele's pines, that told of her faithless lover. The tapering cypress pointed the way to the heavenly Paradise.

Nor was any gift there wanting of all Pomona gives, Nature producing them in their infinite variety without need of cultivation, and far superior in consequence: purple cherries, mulberries, whose Portuguese name, *amoras*, is so close kin to love, the peaches first found in Persia and so greatly improved when grown elsewhere. The bursting pomegranate shone with a redness to outvie the ruby. Jocund vine was interwoven with spreading elm, the grapes hanging in clusters of dark purple and green; and so mightily did the pear-tree flourish that its laden boughs, like pyramids, constrained it to welcome the depredations of the birds.

As for the flowery sward that carpeted the rustic scene, making the shady valley more charming still, its delicate beauty robbed Persia's tapestries of their sheen. The narcissus drooped its head over the clear, motionless pool, and all around grew anemones, telling of that Adonis for love of whom Venus had not yet ceased to pine. With the same colours adorning field and sky, it was in fact hard to tell if it was the flowers that gave the lovely dawn its hues, or the dawn the flowers.

Flora and Zephyr were even then painting with reds and whites – the lovers' colour – violet, iris and marjoram, the lily glistening with the morning dew, the rose whose fresh beauty was like a maiden's cheeks. On the hyacinth's leaves could be read Apollo's *Ai* of grief for the death of its namesake. It was clear from fruits and flowers that Flora and Pomona were in competition.

Overhead, birds filled the air with their song. Animals

frolicked no less joyously on the ground. Along the lake the snow-white swan was singing, and from the bough the nightingale made reply. The stag took no alarm to see its horns mirrored in the crystal depths. Here a swift hare or timid gazelle sprang from the thicket, there a dainty bird winged its way back to the nest with food for its dear ones in its beak.

Such, as these new Argonauts came ashore from their ships, was the cool and charming scene that met their gaze. The lovely goddesses meantime were strolling about the glade as though all unaware. Some were playing sweet music on the zither, some on harp or sonorous flute. Others with golden bow made faint pretence of hunting, for none followed her prey. It was thus their expert instructress had counselled, that they should scatter over the fields and begin by awakening desire in the mariners with the fleeting view of an uncertain prize. Some, trusting to the beauty unadorned of a lovely form, had laid aside the enhancement of attire and were bathing naked.

The stalwart Portuguese, eager to be touching land once more, were now hastening up the beach, not a man of them remaining behind. One attraction was the pleasures of the chase: little did they think that among those enchanting hills there was hunting to be had, without snare or net, as gentle, tame, and accommodating as Venus had there disposed for them. A number, armed with musket and cross-bow, made resolutely for the sombre thickets and glades in search of deer. Others, drawn by the shade that protected from the noonday sun, walked by the banks of streams tripping lightly over their pebbly beds down to the shore.

Then, suddenly, they began to glimpse among the leafy branches a variety of colourings that their eyes persuaded them were, not flowers, but delicate, many-hued fabrics of wool and silk such as human beings, themselves beautiful as the rose, will wear to make their beauty rarer still and incite yet more potently to love.

Veloso in his astonishment gave a great shout. 'Men,' he called, 'what strange game have we here! If it be possible that the ancient pagan cults still persist, this is a glade sacred to the nymphs and we have stumbled on something beyond man's farthest desire. It is obvious that there are greater and more excellent things to be discovered in the world than we unthinking mortals dream of. Let us follow these goddesses and find out if they be real, or only creatures of the imagination.' And with that they all set off, swifter than any deer, and gave chase along the banks.

The nymphs fled through the foliage; but, more cunning than swift, little by little and with many a smile and cry they allowed the hounds to overtake them. As they ran, the breeze caught up now one's golden tresses, now another's delicate drapery, and desire, battening on the sudden glimpse of lovely flesh, grew more ardent still. One stumbled, by design, and her show was rather of complacency than indignation when, as she picked herself up again, her pursuer fell over her and made escape impossible.

Some of his fellows, taking another direction, came upon the nymphs who were bathing naked and drew from them a startled cry, as though such an invasion were the last thing they looked for. Several, feigning a lesser esteem for modesty than for action, rushed as they were into the bush, granting to their pursuers' gaze what they denied their itching hands. One did, indeed, invoke a more maidenly reserve and, swifter even than Diana once in similar case, let the water cover her body; while another snatched hastily at her clothing on the bank.

There was one youth who dashed into the water fully

dressed and booted as he ran, there to quench the fire that
consumed him. Had he stopped to strip, he feared lest that
were not the end of the delay. Wary and astute, and accus-
tomed to fetching the wounded bird out of the water, the
huntsman's dog no sooner sees his master raise the musket
to his cheek to aim at duck or heron than he leaps im-
patiently in, not waiting for the report, and, confident the
bird will fall, swims after it barking. Just so did he make
after his nymph, and found in her no chaste Diana.

Lionardo Ribeiro was a soldier of pleasing presence, re-
sourceful, a good horseman, and ever disposed to fall in
love. Love in truth had dealt him not one but many a re-
buff, ill-treating him so consistently as to bring him to the
firm conviction that in affairs of the heart he had no luck.
He had never wholly abandoned hope, notwithstanding,
that even yet his fate might change.

He, as chance would have it, had singled out Ephyre, a
very paragon of comeliness, but who was determined to
sell more dearly than the others what Nature had given her
to give; and now, exhausted with the pursuit, he called to
her:

'You have vanquished me, you lovely creature, too
lovely to be so cruel. But if you are carrying off my soul,
you might as well wait for the body. All the others have
tired of running and have given themselves up to the
enemy's sweet pleasure. Must you be the only one to keep
on through the thicket, and I the only one still to be
evaded? Who told you it was I who was after you? If it was
that same ill-luck that dogs me wherever I go, I beseech of
you, do not believe it. It has always lied to me whenever I
have put any trust in it, yes, a thousand times an hour.

'Do not wear yourself out: you are tiring me out too.
If you really want to escape from my reach, such is my luck

that even if you were to wait it would prevent my catching you up. So please stop. If that in fact be your desire, I am curious to see what subtle way it will find this time of defrauding me. You need not fear: it will be just the same as always. There is many a slip between the cup and the lip.

'Stop turning your back on me, please, as you would wish Time never to turn his back on your charms. You have only got to check your pace to defeat the harshness of fortune. There is no ruler, no army, powerful enough to master the fury with which it pursues me in all I ever desired; and you can do it single-handed simply by not running away from me.

'Are you going to ally yourself with my ill-fortune? It is a sign of weakness to rally to the stronger side. And why carry off a heart that was free? You will run all the lighter by letting it go. Why weigh yourself down with a soul as wretched as the one you now hold captive in those strands of gleaming gold? Unless, perhaps, since taking it prisoner you have altered its lot and it now weighs less.

'It is in this hope only that I keep on pursuing you, that either you may give way under the burden, or by virtue of your lovely face it may be rescued from its present grim and miserable fate. And if the change is to befall, gentle maiden, do not keep on running away from me; for Love will aim his dart at you, and if he strike, then you must await me. And if you wait, I have nothing more to ask.'

If the lovely nymph still ran on it was not now, as before, to make her downcast pursuer pay dearly for his prize, but that she might still hear his sweet lament and love-lorn plaints. But now, turning to look at him with an expression of benign tenderness, her face wreathed in laughter and tears, she fell to the ground at her victor's feet, and all was forgotten in the ecstasy of love.

What hungry kisses and pretty weeping might then have been heard throughout the glade, what gentle caresses and becoming indignation, that turned straightway to merry, rippling laughter! What more took place those morning and noontide hours, with Venus ever fanning the flames of delight, is rather to be experienced than described. Let him describe who is debarred from the experience.

And now the beauteous nymphs, in perfect harmony with their sailor-lovers, wove dainty chaplets of laurel and gold and a wealth of flowers to deck their brows. Then, bestowing their snow-white hands in marriage, they exchanged solemn, binding promises of such eternal comradeship, good faith and happiness as should last through life and death.

Chief among all the nymphs, she to whom the others owned respectful obedience, was Tethys herself, reputed the daughter of Uranus and Vesta – and from her looks, that dazzled land and sea alike, one could well believe it. She gave her hand to the illustrious da Gama, an honour richly deserved. The act was celebrated with a seemly display of regal pomp, that revealed her as outstanding among the great of her sex.

Explaining to him then who she was, she gave him to understand, in a noble exordium adorned with all the graces of eloquence, that she had come there at the bidding of immutable destiny to unfold to him, through the gift of prophecy, the remaining secrets of the sphere, both lands still untrodden and seas still unsailed, a revelation merited by Portugal alone.

Thereupon she took him by the hand and led him up to the crest of a lofty, sacred mountain where stood a palatial edifice, all finest crystal and purest gold. Here the company spent the greater part of the day in gentle sports and pleasure unalloyed, the queen indulging her love within the palace, the other nymphs without, in shady nooks among the flowers.

And so the stalwarts and their fair brides passed the long hours to nightfall, radiant with a tender happiness they had never known before, that was compensation in full for all their arduous experiences. It is thus that life reserves to the latter end its reward for deeds of outstanding bravery and daring: only when fully earned can it carry with it resounding fame and a great and glorious name.

For Tethys, the so lovely ocean-nymphs, the magic island with its rich colourings, all are but symbols of the honours, delightful in themselves, that can make life sublime. The thrilling exaltation to the heights, the triumphs, the brow garlanded with palm and laurel, the glory and the wonder of it all, these are the island's joys.

The ancients loved greatness, and were wont in imagination to endow with immortality, on the peaks of starry Olympus, the hero who had mounted aloft on the soaring wings of fame, his passport his valorous deeds and the mighty labours that attend the path of virtue, ever a steep and rocky path even though it prove in the end to have its sweets, its joys, and its delights. This was their way of rewarding the sublime, immortal achievements of mortals who in their genius and daring partook of the divine. Jupiter, Mercury, Apollo, Mars, Aeneas, Romulus, Bacchus, Hercules, Ceres, Minerva, Juno, Diana, all in their origin were but frail humanity. It was Fame, trumpeting their exploits abroad, who gave them these strange titles of gods, semi-gods, immortals, tutelary deities, heroes and supermen.

Awaken then, you who set store by fame, if you would be their peers in the world's esteem. Rouse yourselves from the slumber of ignoble lethargy, that reduces the free spirit of man to serfdom. Put a severe curb on covetousness and unworthy ambition alike, that drag you so constantly at their heels; and no less on tyranny, the black and shameful vice that drives as it degrades. Empty honours, tainted gold confer no real distinction. Better deserve and not enjoy them than possess them unearned.

Devote yourselves instead, if not to the task of keeping the country at peace and endowing it with just and firm laws such as confer nothing on the rich that belongs to the poor, then to girding on your shining armour and going out to fight the Saracen. Either way you can make your country great and powerful. Everyone will have more, no one less, and you will have achieved wealth deservedly, and with it the honour that casts such a lustre on existence. You will confer fame no less on the monarch you love so dearly, now through well-considered counsels, now with your strong right arm, and will attain to immortality for yourselves as your fathers did before you.

Count nothing impossible: he who willed always found a way. In the end you too will be listed on fame's scroll of heroes, and this Island of Venus will be yours.

CANTO

10

B UT now the sun was sinking to its setting in the farthest West, where ocean laps the shores of Mexico. A cool breeze had sprung up to temper its ardent rays, its breath rippling the placid waters of the pools and awakening the lilies and jessamines from their torpor. The nymphs, hand in hand with their lovers, a bond of deep content between them, were making their way into the resplendent palace halls, dazzling with the sheen of precious metals.

Tethys had summoned them, having prepared for their delectation and the repair of wearied nature tables spread with an abundance of rare and exquisite dishes; and there the couples sat down, each lover with his bride, on seats of delicate crystal. At the head were two of pure gold, where sat da Gama with his lovely goddess.

Golden platters, brought up from the treasure-houses of the deep, were laden with such dainty and enticing sweetmeats as the famed banquets of ancient Egypt never knew. Fragrant wines, superior not merely to Roman Falernian but to the very ambrosia of Jupiter and his gods, bubbled and foamed in diamond goblets, leapt to the addition of water, then struck a sudden joy to the cockles of the heart.

The conversation turned on a thousand cheerful topics, many a gentle laugh and subtle quip bridging the progress from course to course and whetting their merry appetites. And all the while a siren with a heavenly voice sang to the strains of instruments sweet as Orpheus's lyre itself, that once in the lower regions soothed the torments of the damned. The perfect harmony of voice and accompaniment resounded through the lofty halls.

Suddenly a silence reined in the winds, hushed the waters to a gentle murmur, and lulled the wild beasts asleep in their lairs. For now the nymph's sweet voice was proclaiming to the heavens great heroes still unborn. Their coming Proteus had clearly discerned in a hollow, transparent globe that appeared to him in his dreams – the gift was Jupiter's – and afterwards, down in Neptune's watery domains, he had told it to the others as prophecy, and the nymph had stored the whole heroic story in her memory.

What she had learnt then was matter for the tragic, not the comic, muse, and such as was never vouchsafed to Iopas, Dido's Carthaginian bard, nor to Demodocus of the court of Alcinous the Phaeacian.

And here, Calliope, in this my final labour, I invoke your aid again. Grant me, I beseech of you, in return for what I now seek to write, and seek perhaps in vain, that I may recover the joy of writing, that is beginning to fail me. The years are closing in about me, and soon summer must give way to autumn. Fate's chill hand is descending on my muse, that I no longer boast of with pride, nor can even rely upon. The buffetings of fortune sweep me on towards the dark river of oblivion and eternal sleep. Enable me, great Queen of the Muses, still to accomplish my desire towards my native land.

The nymph was telling in song how from the Tagus, over the ocean da Gama had opened up, fleets would come and conquer those shores laved by the Indian Ocean, and how such pagan rulers as refused to bow the neck to their yoke would feel the weight of their anger and of their strong right arm until finally they surrendered, if not to it, to death.

She sang of one, a king of Cochin and high priest among the people of Malabar, who, rather than break the ties of friendship he had sworn with the doughty Portuguese, would suffer the great Samorin to raze his towns and cities by fire and sword, with a fierceness and cruelty that were the measure of his hatred for the newcomers.

And then she told how, far away in Belem on the Tagus, one would embark who was destined to right the wrong, the great Pacheco Pereira, little dreaming, this Lusitanian Achilles, just how great he was to be. When he stepped on board, vessel and restless ocean alike would feel his weight as the creaking timbers sank beyond their wont.

Arrived at length in distant India and assigned with but a small force to the relief of his pagan ally, Pacheco would inflict a heavy defeat on the accursed Naires in the salty waters of the winding Cochin River, at the Strait of Cambalon; and the sight of so few achieving so much would strike chill dread into the whole mighty hothouse of the East.

The Samorin would send out a call for reinforcements, and kings would rally to him from Bipur and Tanor and from the hills of Narsinga, all assuring the emperor that they would give a good account of themselves. Every Naire from Calicut to Cananor, pagan and Moslem alike, would be bidden take up arms, the Moslems fighting at sea, the others on land.

And the dauntless Pacheco would defeat them all a second time, on land and sea, leaving the whole of Malabar astounded at the scale of the slaughter. Losing no time, the Samorin would attack impetuously yet again, reviling his forces and making vows, in vain, to his vain gods, who would remain unhearing and unmoved.

Then Pacheco, no longer content merely to defend the river-crossings, would set to burning the enemy's villages, temples and houses. And still the dog of an infidel could discover no sign of exhaustion in the foe, for all this arson and pillage. Blazing with anger, he would make his troops attack him at two crossing-places at once, regardless of the cost in lives. But Pacheco would prove to have wings, and flying from one to the other, would once more rout them utterly.

This would bring the Samorin himself to view the battle and encourage his men in person, until a cannon-shot whistling through the air would bespatter him with the blood of its victims in the royal palanquin itself. After that, in despair of making any impression on Pacheco either by force or tactics, he would resort to treachery and poison, and still always in vain, it being the will of Heaven that his resistance should grow steadily less effective.

A seventh time he would come back, the nymph's song went on, to fight the brave, invincible Portuguese, on whom no exertions seemed to weigh or leave their mark; and again, unaided, Pacheco would throw him into confusion. This time he would bring to the encounter wondrous new engines raised on planks from which to hurl grappling-irons at the caravels, that till then he had never been able to attack with any success. He would launch towering sheets of flame upon the water in an attempt to fire the fleet. And, as before, the soldier's skill and ingenuity would hurl back the desperate onslaught.

Of all who have ever won renown in war, however high they may have soared on the pinions of fame, there is none can touch this hero: with due respect to the greatness of

Greece and Rome, he bears away the palm from them all.

The waging of so many battles with such infinite skill and resource, he having little more than a hundred men, the routing of so many dogs not unversed in war, must either seem but a dreamer's imaginings or suggest that the heavenly choir, hearing his prayer, had rallied to his aid and bestowed on him at once courage, strength, wiliness, and a stout heart.

Not Miltiades when he overwhelmed all the might of Darius on the field of Marathon, nor Leonidas with his four thousand Lacedemonians defending the pass of Thermopylae, nor the youthful Ausonian Horatius Cocles as he held the bridge against the entire Etruscan army, nor Quintus Fabius with his war of attrition against Hannibal, is to be compared with him for valour and wisdom in battle.

At this point the nymph muted her song to a melancholy dirge as, in a low voice thick with tears, she sang of the ingratitude with which such bravery was attended. 'O Belisarius,' she wailed, 'whose name the Muses will never cease to exalt, if experience once taught you how far greatness in war can fail of its due reward, here is one from whom you may draw consolation, a meet companion alike in his deeds of prowess and in the harsh injustice that was meted out to him. In you and in him are to be seen to what lowly estate nobility of heart may sink when humbled and forgotten.

'To think that men who have been as a bulwark to their king and faith should die in the wretchedness of a hospital bed! Such is the behaviour of monarchs when caprice takes precedence over justice and truth, when they permit themselves to be carried away by a flattering exterior: the reward that belonged to Ajax they bestow on Ulysses, the fraudulent cajoler. Yet even so there is revenge: for he who gives ear to false adulation may pass by the noble and wise in apportioning his favours, but only to see these disappear straightway into the maw of avarice and sycophancy.

'If you, O King, who made such sorry return to such a vassal – it is the only blemish on your record – were not capable of raising him to an honourable estate, he was of winning for you a wealthy kingdom. As long as the sun goes round the earth, I can assure you that he shall be held great and illustrious among men, and you will stand accused of having treated him scurvilȳ.

'But here,' she continued her song, 'comes another, Francisco de Almeida, bearing the title of Viceroy and accompanied by his son. He will win for himself as great fame on the ocean as any Roman of old ever did. Father and son together will inflict severe chastisement on Kilwa, expelling the treacherous tyrant who rules over it and setting up a loyal and humane king in his place. Mombasa, a city of fine houses and splendid buildings, they will raze to the ground, destroying all its beauty, in punishment for previous misdeeds.

'On reaching the coast of India, the son Lourenço will himself perform wonders with his ships against the swarming enemy and his artifices. Even though the sea be black with the Samorin's great vessels, the thunderous fire of his guns will put them out of action, smashing rudders, masts and sails to pieces. Then, making boldly for the enemy flagship, he will grapple it fast, leap on board, and account for some four hundred Moslems with sword and lance alone.

'At last, in the inscrutable providence of God, that alone can know the wisdom of its measures, Lourenço will find himself in a position where neither courage nor prudence may avail him. For in Chaul, in a fight with the combined fleets of Egypt and Cambay, a fight so bloody and stubborn that it churns the waters, he will lose his life. Only sheer might can prevail against heroic valour, and here the strength of the swarming enemy, a lull in the wind, and the mounting perils of the sea will all be ranged against him.

'Could the heroes of antiquity come back to life, what a lesson in courage and nobility might they not learn from the sight of this second Scaeva who can be cut to pieces but not made to surrender! With the whole of one thigh carried away by a chance cannon-ball, he still fights on with arms undaunted and a heart as stout as iron. At length another shot snaps the links that hold body and soul together, and his soul, taking wing, will leave its earthly prison behind and soar victoriously aloft.

'Go in peace: after the turbulence of war you have earned tranquil repose. As for your mutilated body, your father is already preparing vengeance. Already I can hear the rolling thunder of his guns and blunderbusses as they dispatch the fierce Cambayans and Mamelukes to the nether regions. Here he comes, stupendous in resolve, blind to everything but grief and lust for revenge, his heart on fire and his eyes tear-drenched with a father's love, confident in his noble rage that he will make the enemy vessels run knee-deep with blood. What he has in mind to do will be seen on the Indus, it will be heard on the Ganges and felt on the Nile.

'Like a jealous bull making trial of its strength for the grim combat ahead, testing its horns against lofty oak or beech and emitting piercing roars the while, so Dom Francisco will not descend in fury on the Gulf of Cambay until he has first sharpened his sword on the opulent city of Dabul, humbling its presumptuous daring to the dust.

'From there he will sail to the Bay of Diu, already the scene of famous battles and sieges, and scatter a large if indifferently armed fleet from Calicut that will pin its faith chiefly to its oars. The cautious Egyptian squadron under Malik Yaz will be caught in a hail of cannon-fire and sent to the bottom; while the Cambayan vessels of Mir Husayn, forced by his grapnels to await the avenging wrath of the Portuguese, will see arms and legs tossed on the waves with no bodies to claim them. The victors strike, in their blind fury, like bolts of thunder, and soon there is nothing to be seen or heard save smoke and flames and cries and flashing swords.

'But look: embarking for his native Tagus after this notable triumph, Almeida will come near to losing fame and glory through the mournful and ill-fated event I see looming ahead. The Cape of Storms, that is destined to preserve his memory with his bones, will not hesitate to rob the world of so brave a spirit, something that all the might of Egypt and India could not do. Savage Kaffirs, armed only with rude, fire-hardened clubs, will succeed where experienced enemies failed, for all their bows and cannon. The judgements of God are baffling to man. The superstitious, unable to understand them, talk of ill-luck and black misfortune: the workings of Divine Providence are the true explanation.

'But what great light is this,' sang the nymph, 'that I see flare up yonder in the direction of Malindi, where the sea runs red with the razing of three cities, Lamo, Oja, and Brava? This is the doing of Tristão da Cunha, a name that will never be forgotten throughout the sea that washes these southern islands and the far-famed shores of Madagascar in particular.

'And now I see another light. It comes from the fires and

the flash of arms at Albuquerque's defeat of the Persians of Ormuz, whose bravery in refusing to submit to a light and honourable yoke they will have cause to regret. Hissing arrows will here be seen to turn back in mid-flight against those who shot them, for he who fights to extend the faith of Mother Church will have God on his side. Not all the salt in the nearby salt-hills will suffice to preserve the corpses of the slain that strew the shores and float in the waters of Gerum, Muscat, and Kalyat. In the end the enemy will learn from the sheer physical superiority of the Portuguese to bow the neck, and a heavy tribute in Bahrein pearls will then be exacted from that iniquitous land.

'Now Victory is busy weaving wreaths of palm-leaves to crown the hero's brow after his fearless seizure of the famous island-city of Goa. Later, yielding to severe pressure, he will abandon it again, but only to await a favourable opportunity to return; for fortune and even might of arms can be overthrown by valour and skill.

'See him now as he renews the assault, that neither walls, lances, fire nor cannon-ball can arrest, forcing his way sword in hand through the fearsome serried ranks of pagan and Moslem. It will be St Catherine's Day, and his great-souled warriors will fight there with a fury unmatched by hungry lion or raging bull.

'And still less can Malacca, with its fame and opulence, hope to escape him, even though its wealth lie far removed, in the very lap of the dawn. I see it arming now, but poisoned arrows and daggers will avail it nothing, for sentimental Malays and valiant Javanese shall alike own the sway of Portugal.'

The siren would have continued her song in praise of the illustrious Albuquerque, had she not here remembered a deed of anger that is to weigh heavily on his fame, world-wide though this be. When fate has decreed that a great leader shall win eternal glory through his exploits, he owes it to his men to show himself a kindly companion to them, not a cruel, unbending judge. Where hunger, hardship and sickness, enemy arrows and sizzling shot, season and circumstance are all at their most hostile to soldiers unfaltering in their obedience, it must seem an act of savage brutality, possible only to the inhuman and overweening breast, to pronounce the extreme penalty for a fault that frail humanity and love have ever condoned.

This will be no crime of abominable incest, nor of violence against an innocent maiden, still less of foul adultery, for the woman is but a common, insignificant and lascivious slave. The man who, from jealousy, or prudery, or from over-familiarity with cruelty and violence, fails to curb an insane rage against his own followers, besmirches the lustre of his reputation with a black and ugly stain.

Alexander the Great, on seeing Apelles in love with his fair Campaspe, gave her to him gladly, though he was none of his veterans nor was he sharing with him the rigours of a perilous siege. When Cyrus discovered that Araspas had become passionately enamoured of Panthea, whom he had entrusted to his safe keeping on the assurance that he for one was immune from any woman's charms, he lightly pardoned him, recognizing that against Love, his victor, there was no defence, and had his reward in the notable services Araspas later rendered him. Judith, daughter of Charles the Bald of France, was carried off by Baudouin the Iron-armed and made his wife; yet Charles not merely spared Baudouin's life but, by giving him Flanders to settle, used him to further his own ambitious designs.

The nymph resumed her long story, beginning to sing of Soares de Albergaria, who was to hoist his banner and strike terror all along the shores of the Red Sea. 'Loathsome Medina will come to fear him, and Mecca and Jidda no less, and the farthest strands of Abyssinia. The fate that has already befallen the mart of Zeila will threaten Berbera. Ceylon, the noble island long famous as Taprobana, whose cinnamon-groves fill it today with a sovereign pride, will pay tribute of that same fragrant spice to the might and glory of the Portuguese flag as it flutters triumphant from the fortress of Colombo, enough in itself to inspire a profound respect in the natives.

'Lopes de Sequeira, leading another expedition to the Red Sea, will open up a new route to the great empire of Abyssinia, the boasted home of Candace and the Queen of Sheba. He will visit Massawa, that must rely on cisterns for its water-supply, and the neighbouring port of Arquico, and will be responsible for the discovery of remote islands rich in new wonders for mankind. After him will come Duarte de Meneses, who, having shown his metal first and chiefly in Africa, will chastise haughty Ormuz for its rebellion by doubling its tribute.

'You too, da Gama, in compensation for your exile now, an exile you will shortly repeat, will return one day to rule as Viceroy over the land you have discovered, bearing the title of Count and laden with honours. Death, that fatal term to all mankind, will claim you from the world and its illusions while still invested with the royal dignity, and then a second Meneses will rule.

'Henrique by name, prudent far beyond his years and smiled on by Fortune, he will never be forgotten. Not merely will he defeat the Malabaris, destroying Panane and Coulete after rushing their guns in sublime contempt of the punishing hail: endowed with truly exemplary virtues, he will vanquish too all seven deadly sins, his triumph over cupidity and incontinence at such an age being the very crown of excellence.

'Then for him too the heavenly summons will come, and it will be your turn, brave Mascarenhas. Wicked enemies may oust you from command, but rest assured that your fame will be eternal. And that even they may confess your worth, Fate has resolved that when you come to take up office, though just fortune be absent, the laurels of victory shall already be yours. In the kingdom of Bintan, for so long a thorn in the side of Malacca, such will be the valour of your men that a single day shall see avenged the wrongs of a thousand years. Superhuman toils and perils, narrow channels spiked with countless iron prongs, stockades, earthworks, lances, arrows: I warrant you will vanquish and master them all.

'In India, notwithstanding, covetousness and ambition will make bold to set their faces openly against God and justice and will inflict on you, not shame, for that they cannot, but annoyance. Still, he who through abuse of the power entrusted to him commits foul wrong and unreason is not the victor thereby: true victory lies in upholding justice in all its naked integrity.

'And yet it may not be denied that Vaz de Sampaio, the usurper, will likewise prove outstanding in valour and will come down like a thunderbolt on seas thick with enemy vessels. In Bacanor he will strike a devastating first blow against the might of Malabar, and a second against the now terrified Moslem admiral Cutiale, routing his entire armada.

'As for the dread fleet of Diu, whose size and daring have given the squadron in Chaul cause for apprehension, the mere sight of his lieutenant Heitor da Silveira will destroy it utterly. This Portuguese Hector will himself be remembered as having been no less a flail to the Gujaratis, in their unremitting defence of the coasts of Cambay, than the Trojan was to the Greeks.

'To the valiant Sampaio there will succeed Nuno da Cunha, who will remain at the helm for many years. He is to build the towering fortress of Chale, and to cause Diu itself to tremble. The stronghold of Bassein will surrender to him, though not bloodlessly, for its Moslem governor will there lose his life and the proud defences will only yield to force of arms.

'Next in the succession is Garcia de Noronha, thanks to whom the fierce Turks will be compelled to abandon the siege of Diu, [now in Portuguese hands and] worthily defended by the military experience and bravery of António da Silveira. Death in due course will claim Noronha too, and now it will be a son of your own, da Gama, who will venture on the government of empire. Before his ardour the Red Sea will turn jaundiced with fear.

'From the hands of your Estêvão the reins pass now to one who will already have achieved fame in Brazil, Martim Afonso de Sousa, scourge of French pirates and sea-dogs. Appointed first from Brazil to be Captain-General of the Indian Ocean, under da Cunha, Sousa will scale the fortifications of haughty and strongly-held Daman, whose gates he will be the first to enter in spite of a heavy covering fire of shot and arrows. And it is to him that the infinitely proud king of Cambay will have granted a fort within the rich city of Diu itself, in return for a promise to help defend his sovereignty against the might of the Great Mogul.

'Afterwards, with surpassing bravery, he will halt the advance of the Samorin against an ally of the Portuguese, driving him and all his minions back in a welter of blood. He will destroy the city of Repelim, putting its king and many of his people to flight, and will follow this up with a famous exploit near Cape Comorin, the overwhelming in a ferocious onslaught of the Samorin's principal fleet, that had been confident it could sweep the seas of the world. Nearby Beadala will also feel the weight of his attack.

'Having thus [as Captain-General] cleared India of enemies, there will be neither resistance nor threat of resistance left when later he returns as Viceroy, for all will tremble at his authority, none daring to voice opposition. Baticala alone will invite upon its head the harsh chastisement that has already befallen Beadala: running blood and littered with corpses, reduced to ruins by fire and shelling, it will be an ugly sight. Such will be Martinho, his name like his deeds deriving from Mars himself: as famous in arms wherever he goes as he is sage and prudent in counsel.

'His successor, João de Castro, will prove another unwearying upholder of the standard of Portugal. Worthy in all things of such a predecessor, he will relieve Diu, [besieged a second time,] as doughtily as the other won it. Warlike Persians, Abyssinians, Turks (or Rumes, as they were then called, from their ancient association with Rome), and many another race as motley in features as in dress will add ferocity to the siege, all raising their vain lamentations to the heavens that a mere handful of men should debar them from the land. Blaspheming against their gods, they swear to bathe their curling mustachios in Portuguese blood.

'Within, Mascarenhas and his men are withstanding artillery-fire of every calibre, fearsome catapults, hidden mines, facing joyfully what seems certain death. Then, when the threat is at its direst, Castro the liberator will send his own sons to the relief, prepared to see them lay down their lives as a sacrifice to God and a passport to eternal fame.

'One son, Fernando, a chip of the old block, will be killed at the shattering of a redoubt in a violent mine explosion, his soul taking wing to Heaven. Alvaro, the other, will triumph over the perils of wind and waves, and finally of the enemy, as he forces open a way to the city through seas fearsome winter had made impassable.

'And now here comes the father, ploughing the ocean with the rest of the Portuguese forces to launch an attack so forceful and, more important, so skilful that it issues in a resounding victory. Some of his men, too impatient for gates, shin up the walls; others hack their way through the furious enemy ranks. But deeds so memorable are not to be contained in verse; it would take a lengthy chronicle and more to do them justice.

'After this the intrepid conqueror will go out to meet the powerful king of Cambay in the field, striking terror into his cavalry hordes. Then it will be the turn of Hydal-Khan, who will prove powerless to defend his domains from the avenging arm that falls impartially on Dabul, on the coast, and on Ponda in the interior.

'All these heroes and many another like them, winning their titles to fame and admiration in divers regions, will become as so many Mars among men. And then, their triumphal standards sweeping the seas, they too will come to enjoy the delights of this island, where these same nymphs and this same entertainment will await them, in token of the glory and honour their arduous enterprises have won.'

The nymph ended her song, and her companions all applauded loudly, their cries voicing their happiness in the celebration of such joyous weddings. 'Let the wheel of fortune turn as it will,' they chanted in unison, 'this race of heroes will never lack honour, fame, and glory!'

When all had now satisfied their hunger with the splendid repast, and in the siren's harmonious strains had conjured up the noble deeds therein unfolded, Tethys, radiant in her gracious seriousness, and wishing to enhance the festivities of so glad a day with glories higher still, addressed the blissful da Gama:

'To you, my hero, God in his divine wisdom has granted to see with your bodily eyes what is denied to other mortals, whose vain strivings after knowledge but lead them into error and misery. Follow me, you and your men, with firm and courageous, yet prudent, step up this densely-wooded slope.' And so saying, she led him into a thicket where a mortal might only with extreme difficulty make his way.

Soon they found themselves on a lofty mountain-top, in a meadow studded with emeralds and rubies that proclaimed to the eye it was no earthly ground they trod. And here they beheld, suspended in the air, a globe of such transparency that the light shone right through it and the centre was as visible as the outer surface. What it was made of could not be divined, but it clearly consisted of a series of spheres contrived by the wand of God to rotate about a single fixed centre in such a way that, however they revolved or rose or fell, the whole neither rose nor fell but showed the same from every angle. Its supernatural artifice in short had neither beginning nor ending, but was in all things uniform, perfect, and self-sustained like God its maker.

As da Gama gazed at it he was deeply moved, and stood lost in curiosity and amazement. Then the goddess spoke: 'This thing you see before you is a representation in miniature of the universe, that you may see where your path lies, whither it leads, and what the end of your desires. This is the mighty fabric of creation, ethereal and elemental, as it came from the hand of God who ever was and ever shall be. He envelops this polished globe all about with his being; but what he is, that no man knows, for the human mind cannot soar so high.

'This first sphere that rotates about the other lesser spheres within, and shines with a light so radiant as to blind men's eyes and their imperfect understanding as well, is known as the Empyrean Heaven, wherein the souls of the pure attain to that Supreme Good that is God himself and that he alone can fully comprehend, for his like is not to be found on earth. Here dwell only the true saints in glory. Saturn, Janus, Jupiter, Juno, myself, we are but creatures of fable, figments of man's blindness and self-deception. Our only use is for the turning of agreeable verses; beyond which, all that mankind has been able to do with us comes down to your ingenious baptizing of the stars with our names.

'Since, however, Divine Providence – which among us is symbolized by Jupiter – governs the universe through the great company of the angels (for so the Bible teaches in many of its parables, the good angels guiding and helping man, the evil impeding him all they can), the poet as he seeks now to delight, now to instruct, is taken with the fancy to bestow on these the same names that in their fables the poets of old gave to their gods. The Holy Book itself speaks of the angels of the heavenly choir as gods, and does not deny that this peerless name is also used, wrongly, of the wicked angels. The God of gods, his power being absolute, still works in the universe through secondary agents.

'But to resume the explanation of the Creator's mysterious handiwork. Inside this first motionless sphere of the souls of the blessed is another, the Primum Mobile, that revolves so swiftly its movement escapes the eye. This in its turn has still other spheres within, and by the impressive rapidity of its motion carries them all round with it. That is why the sun, in its precise obedience to a progress not its own, gives us alternate day and night. The nearest to the Primum Mobile of these inner spheres is the Crystalline, that pursues at the same time a slow course of its own, so slow and so severely curbed that the ever-resplendent sun will complete ten-score annual rotations while it takes but a single step.

'Next to this is the sphere of the Fixed Stars, specked with smooth, radiant bodies each endowed with an ordered, scintillating movement about its own axis. You may see clearly how it is garbed and adorned with the long golden belt of the Zodiac, through whose twelve stellar signs, depicted by as many animals, the sun traces its yearly course.

'Look at the pictures the glistening stars evoke. This is Charles's Wain or the Great Bear, this the Little Bear. Here are Andromeda and her father Cepheus, and fearsome Draco. Note how beautiful Cassiopeia is, how turbulent the expression of Orion. These here are Cygnus of the famous swan-song, the Hare and the two Dogs, Argo and the gentle Lyra.

'Immediately within this great firmament you may see the seventh heaven, called after Saturn, the god of antiquity. The sixth revolves under the sign of Jupiter, the next under that of Mars, a warlike enemy. The Sun, that shining eye of the heavens, has its orbit in the fourth sphere. Then come those of Venus, the goddess of love; of Mercury, sovereign in eloquence; and finally of the three-faced goddess known on earth as Diana, in the heavens as the Moon, and in the lower regions as Hecate.

'You will notice how all these spheres have their several movements, some slow, some fast, how now they fly far from their centre and now draw relatively near, in accordance with the design of God Omnipotent who made fire and air, wind and snow, and caused these to lie, as you see here, within the inmost sphere of all, clinging close to earth and sea.

'In this centre is the abode of mankind, who, not content with suffering all the perils of dry land, must needs launch out in its boldness on the restless waters too. Here you may note how, separated by the same tempestuous seas, the various regions are inhabited by different nations under different rulers, with different ways of life and different religions.

'This part is Christian Europe, more advanced and more renowned alike in its governance and its might than the others. Here is Africa, still grasping after the things of this world, uncivilized, full of savagery, with its southern-most Cape [of Good Hope], that has always been denied you until now. Look out over the whole vast continent and see how everywhere it is the home of legions of infidels.

'Observe, here is the great empire of Benomotapa with its naked blacks, where Gonçalo da Silveira is to suffer shame and death for his holy faith. There is abundance of gold, the metal that men most strive after, in this as yet unknown hemisphere. See how the Nile and the Zambezi both have their source in the same lake, and note how the Negroes live in huts without doors, as if they were nests, trusting to the king's justice and to the protection and good faith of their neighbours. Here you can see a brute horde, thick as a cloud of starlings in the sky, assailing the fortress Pero de Nhaia is to build in Sofala, and which he will skilfully defend.

'Look here how the Nile issues from this series of lakes that the ancients never knew. Observe how its crocodile-infested waters irrigate the lands of Abyssinia, with their Christian inhabitants who defend themselves the better from their enemies by the strange device of having no fortifications. Here is Meroe, an island-city famous in earlier times, now called by the natives Noba.

'In this remote region your own son Cristóvão will distinguish himself in arms against the Turks, though there is no fending off death when it comes. And here on the coast is Malindi, that gave you so hospitable and so welcome a reception. Not far off, at Quilmance, you may see the mouth of the Rufiji River, that the natives call in their language the Obi.

'Here is Cape Guardafui, formerly Cape Aromata – both native names – marking the beginning of the approach to the famous Red Sea, whose colour comes from the sea-bed. This serves as boundary between Africa and Asia. On the African side the chief cities are Massawa, Arquico and Suakin. You will notice Suez at the farther end. Of old, they say, it was called, after Heroas, Heroöpolis (others say after Arsinoe). At present it harbours the might of the Egyptian fleets. These are the waters that long ago opened wide to allow Moses to cross, and this is the beginning of Asia, with its vast territories and wealthy kingdoms.

'See here Mount Sinai, ennobled by the tomb of St Catherine, and here Toro, and Jidda, known for its lack of clear spring water. Observe these portals of the Strait of Bab-el-Mandeb, that ends in the parched land of Aden, bordering on the rocky Arzira Mountains where no rains ever fall.

'And here are the three Arabias, their wide expanse entirely peopled by swarthy nomads. This is the home of the

237

thoroughbred so highly esteemed by the warrior for its fire and pace. Note the line of the coast, how it determines here the Strait of Ormuz and projects into Cape Fartak, so called from the well-known city of that name. This is Dofar, renowned as the source of the most aromatic of all altar-incense.

'But look: it is here, just on the other side of Ras el-Hadd with its sterile strands, that the kingdom of Ormuz begins. Its fame will date from the day when the fleet of dread Turkish galleys encounters off its shores the ire of Pedro de Castelo Branco. This next cape is Asaboro, that mariners now call Musandum, at the very entrance to the Persian Gulf, with Arabia on one side and the fertile lands of Persia on the other. And this is Bahrein Island, where the ocean-bed is adorned with rich pearls, their hue the colour of dawn. The Tigris and the Euphrates, joining, here reach the sea together.

'This Persia is a great and noble empire, its people always waging war, for ever in the saddle. They hold it beneath their dignity to fight with cannon, preferring that their hands should be calloused with the wielding of nobler weapons. Observe in this island of Gerum what the passage of time can do. On it once stood the city of Armuza; that vanished, and now a second city, Ormuz, has inherited its name and fame.

'Felipe de Meneses will give proof here of his outstanding bravery in the field when, with a mere handful of Portuguese, he overthrows a large Persian force from Lar. And there are other blows and reverses to come, at the hand of Pedro de Sousa, whose prowess will have been seen earlier in the razing of Ampaza by the sword alone.

'But enough of the Strait of Ormuz and the well-known Ras Jaskah, once called Carpela, whose entire territory –

the Carmania of old – is so ill-favoured that Nature has bestowed on it none of her customary gifts.

'See now the graceful Indus, with its source in yonder height, and the Ganges flowing from another height near by. Look at this extremely fertile land of Sind, and the deep indentation made by the Gulf of Cutch with the sudden inrush of its flood-tide and the impetuous haste with which it ebbs. Cambay, where the sea has again eaten deeply into the coast, is likewise a land fruitful in the extreme. And there are a thousand cities besides that I pass over now, but which are reserved for you Portuguese.

'This celebrated coast of India, as you see, continues to run southward till it ends in Cape Comorin, once Cape Cori, facing Taprobana or Ceylon. Everywhere along these shores Portuguese soldiers still to come will win victories, lands, and cities, and here for long ages they will make their abode. The territories that lie between the two great rivers are beyond compute, and are apportioned among various nations, some Moslem, others pagan, their beliefs deriving from the devil.

'In this kingdom of Narsinga lie the sacred remains of the blessed St Thomas, the same who put his hand into Jesus's side. At the time he arrived here to proclaim the gospel, the pleasant city of Meliapor, once rich and powerful, lay well inland. Its people worshipped the idols of their fathers, as these pagans still do today.

'Thomas had already passed through many lands teaching and preaching, and here he was doing likewise, giving health to the sick and new life to the dead, when it chanced one day that a tree-trunk of enormous size was carried inshore by the waves. The king of Narsinga was then engaged in putting up some new buildings and wanted the tree for timber, not doubting that with his resources in men, elephants and mechanical contrivances he could easily get it to land. But such was its weight that nothing he could do would move it.

'The messenger of the true God needed no such ado. Untying his girdle, he fastened it to the tree-trunk and without effort lifted and pulled it to a spot where he built of it an imposing temple that should stand as an example to future generations. He well knew that, having faith, he had but to command a mountain to move and, deaf though it was, it would straightway obey the sacred injunction. For so God had taught him, and he had already put it to the proof.

'There was great excitement among the people at this. To the Brahmins it came as a revelation, and the more they considered the apostle's miracles and his sanctity the more they feared for their own authority. Envy struck deeper into these pagan priests than it had into any others, and they set themselves in devious ways to prevent his being heard, even if it were to mean putting him to death.

'The chief among them, who wore across his breast the silk and golden strands of office, had resort at length to a fearful deed, from which the world may learn that true virtue has no enemy so cruel-fierce as false. This man slew his own son, and then accused the innocent Thomas of the murder. False witnesses were called, as is the practice, and he was promptly condemned to death.

'Knowing that his only hope lay in his all-powerful Father, the saint decided that now was the time to perform one of his greatest miracles, in the presence of the king and his nobles. He ordered the dead body to be brought in, commanded it to come back to life, and bade them ask the youth himself who killed him, as the one witness no one could refute or disbelieve. And all beheld the youth rise up alive in the name of Christ crucified; and when he had thanked Thomas for restoring his life, he revealed that the murderer was his father.

'So great was the fear this miracle caused that the king was baptized there and then, and many more after him. Some kissed the saint's cloak, others sang the praises of his God. As for the Brahmins, they were consumed with such a renewal of hatred, so poisonous was the envy that gnawed at them, that they made up their minds to do away with him once and for all, and succeeded in persuading the ignorant populace to this end.

'One day, accordingly, as Thomas was preaching to the people, the priests contrived a disturbance in their midst. Christ had already forewarned Thomas that it was his will he should now suffer martyrdom and be lifted up to Heaven, and when his enemies rained stones upon him he offered no resistance. One of the evil-doers, the more quickly to sate his cruelty, thrust a lance into his heart.

'The Ganges and the Indus wept for you, Thomas, as did every land you had ever visited. Those souls who were garbing themselves in the holy faith you had taught them wept more bitterly still. But the heavenly angels sang and rejoiced as they received you into the glory you had won. We ask your intercession of God that he may enable you to show favour to your Portuguese.

'As for you others who usurp the name of God's mission-ers, that Thomas bore, tell me: if you be his envoys, how comes it that you sit at home instead of going forth to preach the holy faith? If, being the salt of the earth, you corrupt yourselves in your own country, where no man is a prophet, wherewith – not to mention the infidels – shall even the heresies be salted that so abound in our time?

'But this is a dangerous theme, and I pass it over. Let us return to our globe with its picture of the coast-line. Here, by this same illustrious city of Meliapor, it begins to curve into the Bay of Bengal. We pass out of the great and wealthy kingdom of Narsinga now, and into Orissa with its busy looms. Where the curve goes deepest the famous Ganges enters the sea. The natives here all bathe in its waters before they die, being persuaded that so their sins, however great, will be washed away and they will be purified. This is Chittagong, one of the finest cities in all Bengal, a land that boasts of its abundance.

'Notice now how the coast swings round and heads once more to the south. This is the kingdom of Arakan, and this Pegu, once peopled with the monstrous breed of its solitary first inhabitants, a woman and a dog. The men here wear small tinkling bells on their genitals, a subtly effective measure introduced by one of their queens against the unspeakable sin.

'The city of Tavoy marks the beginning of the great empire of Siam. Tenasserim comes next, and then Kedah, the chief centre for the production of pepper in these parts, though far from the only one. Farther on lies Malacca, that your countrymen will make known as a great emporium for the wealth and merchandise of all the territories bordering on this vast ocean.

'This noble island of Sumatra was said in ancient times to be joined to the mainland, until ocean breakers eating into the coast drove a wedge between. The Chersonese, the region was called, to which was added the adjective "Golden" from its valuable seams of the metal. Some have imagined it to be the site of Solomon's Ophir. And here, on the very tip of this peninsula, lies Singapore, where vessels find their passage narrowed to a strait.

'The coast now curves north again, and then eastwards, and you can see the kingdoms of Pahang and Patani and the long extent of Siam, to which they and others are subject. This is the River Menam, that rises in the great Lake Chiamai.

'And here now is a vast territory dotted, as you can see, with the names of a thousand nations you have never even heard of: the Laos, powerful in extent and in numbers, the Avas and Bramas, who have their homes in great mountain-ranges, the Karens, savage tribes inhabiting the remoter hills who eat the flesh of their enemies and cruelly tattoo their own with red-hot irons.

'Through Cambodia, you will observe, flows the Mekong River, its name meaning "prince of waters". Like the chilly Nile, it floods even in summer from the volume of its tributaries, turning great stretches of country into lakes and causing much anxiety. The inhabitants of these parts believe in their ignorance that for the entire animal creation there exist a heaven and a hell after death.'

It is here, on the gentle bosom of this same kindly river, that the soaking Cantos of this poem will make harbour after the misery and wretchedness of shipwreck, having survived storms and shallows, privations and perils in compliance with the unjust decree pronounced on one whose harmonious lyre is destined to bring him rather fame than fortune.

The goddess continued: 'This part of the coast is known as Tsian-Pa; in its forests grows the sweet-smelling aloe. Here you may see Cochin-China, still but little known, and Hainan, in the as yet undiscovered Gulf of Tongking.

'And now you are looking at the mighty empire of China, that boasts greater territories and riches than it knows of, its sway reaching from the tropics to the frigid zone. Observe this Great Wall, an incredible thing to build as frontier between one empire and another, proof incontestable and accepted by all of its sovereign power, its pride and wealth. The emperor of the Chinese is not born a prince, nor does the office descend from father to son: he is elected by the people for his outstanding wisdom, virtue, and nobility.

'There is much more of the earth's surface that must still remain hidden from you: in its proper time it shall all be revealed. But do not forget these islands where Nature has chosen to show her greatest wonders. This, that you can only half distinguish where it lies far out to sea, facing China – it is from China that it is to be sought – is Japan, famous for its fine silver, and soon to be famous too through the spreading of Christianity among its people.

'And there are other countless islands, as you see, scattered over the seas of the East. Here is Tidor, and here Ternate, with its volcano spurting columns of fire. You can recognize the clove-trees, that Portugal must still pay for with her blood. This is the abode of the bird of paradise, which never alights on the ground and is only to be found dead. These others are the Banda Islands, gay with the many-hued flower of the nutmeg, from which the numerous species of birds exact their tribute. And here is Borneo, where the trees shed tear-drops of a thick, resinous substance known as camphor, that has made the name of the island famous.

'Yonder lies Timor with its aromatic and health-giving sandalwood. And yonder Java, so large that the southern, more mountainous part has not yet been explored. The natives of the interior say there is a river there with miraculous qualities: provided its waters be not mingled with those of another, it will petrify any piece of wood that falls into it.

'And now we are back to Sumatra, that has only become

an island with time. Here too volcanoes erupt vapour and quivering flames, and you can see a spring that runs oil, and the strange spectacle of a tree weeping tears of fragrant benzoin, more fragrant than all the myrrh of Arabia. And note that this island, that lacks nothing to be found in others, produces also delicate silk and fine gold. In Ceylon observe this mountain, Adam's Peak, so high it overtops the clouds, or so it seems. The natives hold it sacred by reason of a rock on it that bears the imprint of a human foot.

'It is in the Maldive Islands that the stately coco-palm is found growing under the water, its fruit being esteemed an excellent antidote to poison. And here, opposite the strait leading to the Red Sea, is Socotra, famous for its bitter aloes. There are still other islands in this sea, likewise subject to your country, that washes the sandy shores of Africa, where the valuable and little-known ambergris is found, its perfume the rarest of all. And see here the famous island of São Lourenço, that some call Madagascar.

'Such are the new regions of the East that you Portuguese are now adding to the known world by throwing open the gates of the mighty ocean over which you sail with such fortitude. But it is fitting that you should glance too at one achievement in the West of another of your race who, offended with his monarch, will blaze [under an alien flag] such a trail as none had ever thought of.

'You see this vast expanse of land stretching from the farthest north to the opposite pole, that is destined to become famous for its mines of gleaming gold. To your friendly neighbour, Castile, is to fall the distinction of submitting its uncouth neck to her yoke. There are many different countries there, peopled by different races each with its own rites and customs.

'But here, where it broadens out most, Portugal too will have her share, in the region known from its red brazil-wood as Brazil. The very next Portuguese fleet to sail will discover it, and you will call the land at first Santa Cruz.

'And it is along this coast, in search of its farthest extremity, that Magalhães will sail, a true Portuguese in the under-taking if not in allegiance. Rather more than half-way from equator to South Pole he will come on a land, Patagonia, where the inhabitants are of almost gigantic stature; then, farther on, he will discover the strait that now bears his name, which leads to another sea and another land, that Terra Incognita over which the South spreads its icy wings.

'Thus far, O Portuguese, it is granted to you to glimpse into the future and to know the exploits that await your stout-hearted compatriots on the ocean that, thanks to you, is now no longer unknown. And now, having learnt of labours that are to commend you still more strongly to these nymphs, your lovely and ever-loving wives, who are busy weaving for you wreaths of glory, you may take to your ships once again, with a tranquil sea and a following wind to speed you back to your beloved land.'

So spoke Tethys to da Gama; and from that joyous lovers' isle they set sail straightway, bearing with them noble provision of refreshment, bearing too the delectable company of the nymphs, never, for so long as the sun shall shine on mankind, to lose it more.

The sea ever calm, the wind blowing ever gently, they continued on their way until at length the land of their birth, the land they had never ceased to long for, came once more in sight. Sailing up the mouth of the friendly Tagus, they conveyed to their country and to the king they so loved and respected the reward and the glory he had

charged them to seek, adding to his titles the lustre of others
more illustrious still.

*And now, my Muse, let there be an end; for my lyre is no
longer attuned and my voice grows hoarse, not from my song, but
from seeing that those to whom I sing are become hard of hearing
and hard of heart. This country of mine is made over to lusting
greed, its sense of values eclipsed in an austerity of gloom and
depression: there is no longer to be had from it that recognition
which fans the flame of genius as nothing else can. And I know
not by what turn of destiny it should have lost the sense of joyous
pride and pervasive pleasure that buoys up man's spirit to face
toils and travails with unfailing cheerfulness.*

*I appeal to you, my King, who occupy your throne in further-
ance of the divine will. Look round at other peoples and reflect on
the excellence of these vassals who call you their lord. Observe
how cheerfully they go forth on their various ways, spirited as
lions and brave as bulls, exposing themselves to privations and
vigils, to fire and sword, to arrows and cannon-balls, to burning
heat and devastating cold, to the blows of idolaters and Moslems,
to shipwreck and the denizens of the deep, to all the uncharted
perils of the universe.*

*Prepared for any sacrifice in your service, unswerving in
obedience to their so distant king, receiving with a ready and
unquestioning alacrity your every command, however harsh:
with the knowledge that your eye is upon them they will attack
in your name the very devils of hell, and I doubt not but they will
make you the victor, not the vanquished, in the struggle.*

*Do not withhold your favour from them. Gladden them with
your presence and with the gracious humanity of your treatment.
Lighten the rigour of the laws that weigh on them. It is thus that
the road to saintliness is opened. Reward experience when it goes
hand in hand with virtue by appointment to your counsels, for*

these are the men who know the how, the when and the whence things fall to be done.

Favour all men in their several professions, in accordance with the talent they show for them. Let those who are vowed to religion engage regularly in prayers for your regime and seek with penance and fasting to hold vice in check. Ambition let them renounce as but an empty wind, for the good and true religious does not pursue futile glory or riches.

As for those who are vowed to knighthood, hold such in high esteem, for their fervour and intrepidity extend the frontiers not merely of the true faith but of this great empire of yours as well. Remember that they who venture so diligently to such distant climes in your service have two foes to vanquish, first their enemies in the flesh, then, still more redoubtable, extremes of travail.

Let Your Majesty so act that admiring Germans, Frenchmen, Italians, English may never be able to say that the Portuguese are a people rather to be commanded than to command. Take counsel only from such as have lived long and intensely and seen a great deal of life. Those who have studied may know much; the man of experience knows more, and to more purpose. Be reminded how Hannibal scoffed at Phormio, the elegant philosopher, for his long-winded discourse in his presence on the art of war. The discipline of arms is of great importance, Your Majesty: it is not to be studied in the imagination, in fanciful dreams or in poring over books, but in the field, observing, handling its problems, fighting.

But who am I to speak, whose humble condition and upbringing have prevented my ever coming to your knowledge? And yet I know that it is in the mouths of those of lowly estate, at times, that the perfection of tribute is to be found. My life has not lacked serious study, mingled with a wealth of experience; nor, as you may here observe, do I want literary aptitude: qualities all that are rarely to be found together. In your service, a right arm inured to battle; in your praise, a mind devoted to the Muses: all I still need is to be found acceptable in your eyes, where worth ought to meet with esteem.

Should Heaven grant me so much, and should you too one day be moved to embark on an enterprise meet for celebration in song, as something within me, noting the Heaven-sent trend of your designs, whispers prophetically you will, then, whether it be Mount Atlas that comes to dread the mere sight of you more than did Atlas himself the Gorgon's head, or whether, attacking by way of Cape Espartel, you level the fortifications of Morocco and Tarudant, I warrant you that this my Muse, become joyous again with recognition, shall so sing your praises to all mankind that you will be in their eyes a second Alexander, without cause this time to envy Achilles his good fortune in being immortalized by Homer.

THE END

Discover more about our forthcoming books through Penguin's FREE newspaper...

Penguin

It's packed with:

- exciting features
- author interviews
- previews & reviews
- books from your favourite films & TV series
- exclusive competitions & much, much more...

Write off for your free copy today to:
Dept JC
Penguin Books Ltd
FREEPOST
West Drayton
Middlesex
UB7 0BR
NO STAMP REQUIRED

READ MORE IN PENGUIN

In every corner of the world, on every subject under the sun, Penguin represents quality and variety – the very best in publishing today.

For complete information about books available from Penguin – including Puffins, Penguin Classics and Arkana – and how to order them, write to us at the appropriate address below. Please note that for copyright reasons the selection of books varies from country to country.

In the United Kingdom: Please write to *Dept. JC, Penguin Books Ltd, FREEPOST, West Drayton, Middlesex UB7 OBR*

If you have any difficulty in obtaining a title, please send your order with the correct money, plus ten per cent for postage and packaging, to *PO Box No. 11, West Drayton, Middlesex UB7 OBR*

In the United States: Please write to *Penguin USA Inc., 375 Hudson Street, New York, NY 10014*

In Canada: Please write to *Penguin Books Canada Ltd, 10 Alcorn Avenue, Suite 300, Toronto, Ontario M4V 3B2*

In Australia: Please write to *Penguin Books Australia Ltd, 487 Maroondah Highway, Ringwood, Victoria 3134*

In New Zealand: Please write to *Penguin Books (NZ) Ltd,182–190 Wairau Road, Private Bag, Takapuna, Auckland 9*

In India: Please write to *Penguin Books India Pvt Ltd, 706 Eros Apartments, 56 Nehru Place, New Delhi 110 019*

In the Netherlands: Please write to *Penguin Books Netherlands B.V., Keizersgracht 231 NL–1016 DV Amsterdam*

In Germany: Please write to *Penguin Books Deutschland GmbH, Friedrichstrasse 10–12, W–6000 Frankfurt/Main 1*

In Spain: Please write to *Penguin Books S. A., C. San Bernardo 117–6° E–28015 Madrid*

In Italy: Please write to *Penguin Italia s.r.l., Via Felice Casati 20, I–20124 Milano*

In France: Please write to *Penguin France S. A., 17 rue Lejeune, F–31000 Toulouse*

In Japan: Please write to *Penguin Books Japan, Ishikiribashi Building, 2–5–4, Suido, Bunkyo-ku, Tokyo 112*

In Greece: Please write to *Penguin Hellas Ltd, Dimocritou 3, GR–106 71 Athens*

In South Africa: Please write to *Longman Penguin Southern Africa (Pty) Ltd, Private Bag X08, Bertsham 2013*

READ MORE IN PENGUIN

A CHOICE OF CLASSICS

St Anselm	**The Prayers and Meditations**
St Augustine	**The Confessions**
Bede	**Ecclesiastical History of the English People**
Geoffrey Chaucer	**The Canterbury Tales**
	Love Visions
	Troilus and Criseyde
Marie de France	**The Lais of Marie de France**
Jean Froissart	**The Chronicles**
Geoffrey of Monmouth	**The History of the Kings of Britain**
Gerald of Wales	**History and Topography of Ireland**
	The Journey through Wales and **The Description of Wales**
Gregory of Tours	**The History of the Franks**
Robert Henryson	**The Testament of Cresseid and Other Poems**
Walter Hilton	**The Ladder of Perfection**
Julian of Norwich	**Revelations of Divine Love**
Thomas à Kempis	**The Imitation of Christ**
William Langland	**Piers the Ploughman**
Sir John Mandeville	**The Travels of Sir John Mandeville**
Marguerite de Navarre	**The Heptameron**
Christine de Pisan	**The Treasure of the City of Ladies**
Chrétien de Troyes	**Arthurian Romances**
Marco Polo	**The Travels**
Richard Rolle	**The Fire of Love**
François Villon	**Selected Poems**

READ MORE IN PENGUIN

A CHOICE OF CLASSICS

ANTHOLOGIES AND ANONYMOUS WORKS

The Age of Bede
Alfred the Great
Beowulf
A Celtic Miscellany
The Cloud of Unknowing and Other Works
The Death of King Arthur
The Earliest English Poems
Early Irish Myths and Sagas
Egil's Saga
The Letters of Abelard and Heloise
Medieval English Verse
Njal's Saga
Roman Poets of the Early Empire
Seven Viking Romances
Sir Gawain and the Green Knight

READ MORE IN PENGUIN

A CHOICE OF CLASSICS

Leopoldo Alas	**La Regenta**
Leon B. Alberti	**On Painting**
Ludovico Ariosto	**Orlando Furioso** (in 2 volumes)
Giovanni Boccaccio	**The Decameron**
Baldassar Castiglione	**The Book of the Courtier**
Benvenuto Cellini	**Autobiography**
Miguel de Cervantes	**Don Quixote**
	Exemplary Stories
Dante	**The Divine Comedy** (in 3 volumes)
	La Vita Nuova
Bernal Diaz	**The Conquest of New Spain**
Carlo Goldoni	**Four Comedies (The Venetian Twins/The Artful Widow/Mirandolina/The Superior Residence)**
Niccolò Machiavelli	**The Discourses**
	The Prince
Alessandro Manzoni	**The Betrothed**
Emilia Pardo Bazán	**The House of Ulloa**
Benito Pérez Galdós	**Fortunata and Jacinta**
Giorgio Vasari	**Lives of the Artists** (in 2 volumes)

and

Five Italian Renaissance Comedies
(Machiavelli/**The Mandragola**; Ariosto/**Lena**; Aretino/**The Stablemaster**; GI'Intronati/**The Deceived**; Guarini/**The Faithful Shepherd**)
The Poem of the Cid
Two Spanish Picaresque Novels
(Anon/**Lazarillo de Tormes**; de Quevedo/**The Swindler**)